AUSTRALIAN HOMESCHOOLING SERIES

T0363261

English Handbook

Years 1–12

CORONEOS PUBLICATIONS

Item No 567

This book is available from recognised booksellers or contact:

Coroneos Publications

Telephone: (02) 9838 9265   **Facsimile:** (02) 9838 8982
Business Address: 2/195 Prospect Highway Seven Hills 2147
Website: www.coroneos.com.au
E-mail: info@fivesenseseducation.com.au

Item # 567
English Handbook
by Valerie Marett and Carmel Musumeci
First published 2019

ISBN: 978-1-922034-76-2
© Valerie Marett and Carmel Musumeci

Contents

Grammar Rules

Spelling Rules

Writing Reference

Grammar Dictionary

Adjectives

Adjectives may be divided into six main classes:3

1. Descriptive
   - ◆ *The <u>large</u> dog ran* - a general description of the person or thing described by the noun.
2. Demonstrative
   - ◆ *<u>This</u> is my house.*
3. Interrogative
   - ◆ *<u>What</u> time is it?*
4. Possessive
   - ◆ *<u>My</u> hat is in <u>my</u> locker.*
5. Numerical
   - ◆ *We have <u>five</u> dogs.*
6. Distributive
   - ◆ *<u>Every</u> person is able to learn.*

Adjectives tell us more about a person, place or thing (a noun). They tell us what kind, which, what colour and how many. They add interest. They should not be overused.

- ◆ *I have five, juicy oranges.*

Adjective - degrees of

The three degrees of adjectives are: positive, comparative and superlative. To make most adjectives comparative or superlative add **er** or **est**.

- ◆ *The **green** grass grew in abundance. (positive)*
- ◆ *The **greener** grass has had more water. (comparative)*
- ◆ *My grass is the **greenest** grass. (superlative)*

Some adjectives require **more** or **most**.

- ◆ *beautiful, more beautiful, most beautiful.*
- ◆ *Do not add **more** if you have added **er** or **est**.*

A few adjectives are irregular.

- ◆ *good, better, best.*

Adjective - descriptive

A descriptive adjective describes a person or thing. "Handsome" is a descriptive adjective.

- ◆ *The <u>handsome</u> man.*

Adjectives -forming

To form adjectives we use the following suffixes:
-ful, -lent, -ous, -ose, -some, -y (meaning "full of")
-al, -an, -ar, -esque, -ic, -tic, -ile, -ine
  (meaning "like" or "connected with")
-able, -ible, -ble, -bile (meaning "able" or "able to be")
-less (meaning "without" or "lacking")
-en, -n (meaning "made of")
-ish, -ch (meaning "something like or showing nationality")

- ◆ e.g., **-ful**, Jane is very cheerful today.
- ◆ e.g., **-ile** Tactile learning is ideal for small children.
- ◆ e.g., **-able** My team is capable of coping with any task.
- ◆ e.g., **-less** Before the fire engine arrived the situation seemed hopeless.
- ◆ e.g., **-en** That wooden boat will make a perfect birthday present.
- ◆ e.g., **-ish** The sea was rough and her face had a greenish tinge.

Adjective
- comparative
superlative

The **comparative** form of an adjective compares two things. The **superlative** form of an adjective compares three or more things and describes the best or the most.

To make most adjectives comparative or superlative add **"er" or "est".**

- ◆ **add "er" for the comparative,** e.g., larger, **and "est" for the superlative,** e.g., largest.

In the case of words with a consonant, vowel consonant pattern double the consonant and add "er" or "est."

- ◆ wet becomes wetter or wettest, big becomes bigger or biggest.

In the case of a word ending in y, delete the y and add "ier" or "iest."

- ◆ pretty becomes prettier or prettiest.

In the case of words of more than two syllables write "more" or "most" before the word.

- ◆ comfortable becomes more comfortable or most comfortable.
- ◆ beautiful becomes more beautiful, most beautiful.

The exceptions are **good, bad, many/much, little/few, far and old.**

- ◆ old, older, eldest.

Adjective
- demonstrative

point out, or demonstrate the noun or pronoun that they qualify, They are **this, that, these, those, such and "same".**

- ◆ *This is my house.*

Adjective
- distributive

Distributive adjectives refer to separate things,

- ◆ **Every** person is able to learn although some learn slower than others.

Distributive adjectives are: **each, every, either** and **neither.**

◆ Each child present will receive a prize.

**Adjective
- indefinite**

Indefinite adjectives refer to numbers but do not say how many.

The most common indefinite adjectives are:
all, any, few, many, several, some

◆ **All** *the people who came to the fair enjoyed themselves.*

**Adjective
- interrogative**

Interrogative adjectives are adjectives which ask questions.

They ask **which, what** and **where.**

◆ **What** *time is it?*

**Adjectives
- numerical**

Numerical adjectives describe the number or numerical order of things.

◆ *Jane invited* **thirty** *people to her birthday.*

**Adjectival
phrases**

add meaning to or describe nouns or pronouns. They may begin with a preposition or present or past participle.

◆ e.g., The boy **near me** was reading a book.
near me—adjectival phrase

◆ e.g., The lady, **waiting near the stairs,** has just arrived.
waiting near the stairs— adjectival phrase

**Adjectives
- Possesive**

show possession, or ownership, but are followed by a noun, My, his, her, its, our, your, their are possessive adjectives.

◆ *My hat is in my locker.*

Adverbs

Adverbs modify verbs, adjectives and other adverbs. They add to the meaning of the word they modify. They tell **how, when, where, why**.

Adverbs tell you how, when or where. They describe the manner, the place and the time. They add meaning to a verb. Many, but not all, adverbs end in **ly**.

The most common types of adverbs are:

manner: *eagerly, happily, quickly, slowly*

time: *always, now, soon, then, later*

place: *here, there, everywhere, up, down, away*

reason: *therefore, consequently, accordingly*

degree: *almost, nearly, quite, rather, much, especially*

negation: *not, never*

interrogation: *how, when, where, why* (when used to ask a question)

- ◆ *Joel happily rode to the shops to collect the paper.* (Manner)
- ◆ *Go now and get that book.* (Time)
- ◆ *Put the cake down here.* (Place)
- ◆ *You did not behave therefore you can not go out.* (Reason)
- ◆ *Never slice the meat unless the safety guard is down.* (Negation)
- ◆ *Where are you going?* (Interrogation)

Adverbial clauses

Adverbial clauses are subordinate clauses which do the work of adverbs. They add meaning to verbs, adverbs or adjectives. Like adverbs they tell how, when, where and why. Adverbial clauses are often referred to as clauses of manner, time, place and reasons.

- ◆ Bob walked <u>where the road is cleanest</u>. (where) place
- ◆ Mr Smith was sleeping <u>when we arrived</u>. (when) time
- ◆ My friend weeded the garden <u>as he was told</u>. (how) manner
- ◆ You will find the pattern difficult unless <u>you are an experienced knitter</u>. (why) reason

Adverbial phrases

Adverbial phrases add meaning to a verb.
They tell how, where, when or why.

- ◆ My friend always arrives on time.
  on time tells when she arrives.

A phrase may begin with a preposition or an infinitive. An infinitive is the verb without any reference to the subject. It can not act as a complete verb in a sentence and is usually proceeded by to.

- ◆ The girl ran <u>with great speed</u>. (with is the preposition)
- ◆ I beeped the horn <u>to startle the cat</u> that lay on the road. (infinitive)

Alliteration	**Alliteration** is the systemic repetition of the same sound in a piece of writing, to produce an effect, sometimes humorous.
Anagram	An anagram is a word that is made up of the letters of another word, i.e., when a word has its letters rearranged to make a new word with no letters missing and no letters added. ◆ The anagram of **act** is **cat**.
Antonyms	Words that have the opposite meaning are called antonyms. ◆ *The opposite of <u>vigilant</u> is <u>heedless</u>.*
Antithesis	**Antithesis** is any arrangement of words to emphasise the meaning by contrast. ◆ Man proposes, God disposes
Apostrophes - ownership	An apostrophe is used to indicate possession, that is to show that something belongs to someone else. ◆ *The <u>mother's</u> chair.* Sometimes a group of words are written differently but can be better written using an apostrophe. ◆ *The home of the family* **or** *the family's home* Sometimes when two words are joined together, the word is shortened and an apostrophe, a raised comma, is used to show that one or more letters is missed out. <u>did not</u> becomes <u>didn't</u>.
Argument or persuasive essay	The purpose of an argumentative or persuasive essay is for a person to present a point of view. It is organised into: ◆ *a statement of position* ◆ *the argument backed up by evidence* ◆ *a summing up and conclusion* ◆ *a call for some action*
Articles	There are only three articles: **a, an** and **the**. **Articles** describe nouns and are adjectives as well as articles.

Article **- definite**	**the** is called a **definite article** because it refers to only one thing. ◆ *The man means one particular man.*
Articles **- indefinite**	**a** and **an** are **indefinite articles** because they do not point to only one specific thing. ◆ *I have an orange.* ◆ *I took the dog for a walk.* **an** is used when the word following begins with a vowel (a, e, i, o, u, h). ◆ *I would like an egg.*
Brackets	**Brackets**, also called **parentheses**, are always used in pairs. They enclose extra information in the form of an example, a comment or an explanation. The bracket helps clarify or add to the information. Eat a green vegetable, (spinach, beans or peas,) each day. Brackets are also used to set off numbers or letters in an outline or list. ◆ *(1) Jot down ideas* *(2) Put them into a logical order*
Capital letters	**Capital letters** are used to begin sentences; for names; for titles; for countries, and towns; for days and months; for titles of books and poems (for proper nouns). When writing direct speech, a capital letter is used at the beginning of the spoken words that are in quotation marks. In abbreviations, words are shortened and a full stop is added to show there is part of the word missing. For example, min. = minutes. When peoples' titles and occupations are abbreviated they always finish with a full stop, unless the first and last letter of the word are used in the abbreviation. For example, Mister Brown becomes Mr Brown. If a name is made up of more than one word that is shortened, the first letter of each word is used. Some like NSW will have no full stop. Others like B.A. (Bachelor of Arts) will.
Clause	A **clause** is a group of words that contains a finite verb and its subject. A **principal clause** is a clause that makes sense by itself. To find a finite verb you first find the verb and then ask who or what in front of them. ◆ Dogs bark. bark is the verb and dog the subject. Remember that, like a sentence, a clause has a **subject** and **predicate** because it always has a main verb.

◆ The man came to our rescue when we asked for help.

The man (subject), came to our rescue (predicate)
we (subject), (when) asked for help (predicate)

Clause -adjectival

An **adjectival clause** is a subordinate clause which adds meaning to a noun. It does the work of an adjective.

◆ A man who has plenty of money should give generously.
A man should give generously. - main clause
(A man) has plenty of money. - subordinate clause
The subordinate clause describes the man so is an adjectival clause.

Clause -adverbial

Adverbial clauses are subordinate clauses which do the work of adverbs. They add meaning to verbs, adverbs or adjectives. Like adverbs they tell how, when, where and why. Adverbial Clauses are often referred to as clauses of manner, time, place and reasons.

◆ Bob walked <u>where the road is cleanest</u>. (where) place
◆ Mr Smith was sleeping <u>when we arrived</u>. (when) time
◆ My friend weeded the garden <u>as he was told</u>. (how) manner
◆ You will find the pattern difficult <u>unless you are an experienced knitter</u>. (why) reason

Clause - subordinate

A **subordinate clause** adds meaning to a principal clause.

◆ When the rain ceased we hurried home.
we hurried home - principal clause
When the rain ceased - subordinate clause

Colloquialism

Colloquialism is a word or expression not used in formal speech or writing but usually chosen from slang and are generally used within limited areas.

◆ *Game as Ned Kelly.*

Colon

The **colon** indicates a division in writing. It suggests a pause in speech, greater than that of a comma, but less than that of a full stop. It generally separates a general introductory item from a specific explanation, list, phrase, or clause.

◆ *Bob is good at the following sports: cricket, tennis and swimming.*

A **colon** is used after a statement that introduces a statement.

◆ *I have three objections to the plan: it would take too long, cost too much and be too dangerous.*

A colon is also often used to separate the hours from the minutes.

◆ *4:57 instead of three minutes to five o'clock.*

Comma

A **comma** is used in a sentence to give a short pause and to make the meaning clearer. It can be used to separate two words, or groups of words in a sentence to make the meaning clearer.

◆ My best friends are Peter, Frank and David.

◆ I need to pick the tomatoes, beans, corn and capsicum.

Commas are also used to break up dates, times and numbers.

◆ My wife was born on 5th March, 1951.

Cliché

Cliché is any stale or overworked expression.

◆ good as gold

Compound words

Compound words are two words that have been joined together to form a single word.

◆ *arm + chair = armchair.*

◆ *bush + ranger = bush ranger*

◆ *earth + quake = earthquake*

◆ *worth + while = worth while*

Conjunctions

A conjunction is a joining word. It joins words, groups of words or sentences.

The most common conjunctions are **and, or, but, for, nor, so, yet, if, because, while, as, before**. As a general rule, do not start a sentence with a conjunction especially **and, but or because**.

◆ *Jillian went to the zoo, but Barbara didn't.*

Contractions

A **contraction** is two words that have been shortened to one by leaving out a letter or letters and inserting an apostrophe instead.

◆ *I have* becomes *I've.*

Couplet

a **couplet** is any two lines or rhyming verse, especially of equal length.

Dashes	**Dashes** may be used as punctuation marks, or used to indicate an omission of letters or words.
	◆ *Mrs S_____, who is accused of stealing, has left town.* (omission)
	◆ *Mountain air is extremely invigorating - as long as you have good lungs.*
	Dashes are also used between numbers or words to mean until or through.
	◆ *Captain Cook, who lived from 1728-1779, was the captain who discovered the east coast of Australia.*
Double negatives	Do not use two negative words in a sentence.
	◆ *I don't know nothing.* (This is incorrect because it means that you do know something!)
	◆ *I don't know anything.* (correct)
Epitaph	**Epitaph** is an inscription on a tombstone.
	◆ Rest in peace
Explanation	The purpose of an **explanation** is to explain how or why something works.
	The text of an explanation is organised into a generalised statement of the topic and details of how or why set out in paragraphs.
Exclamation marks	**Exclamation marks** are used to show strong feeling or surprise. They are used at the end of a sentence to emphasis some special meaning.
	◆ I don't believe it!
	◆ Help!
Fable	A Fable is a short story used to teach a moral. Aesop's Fables are the most famous of all fables.
Fragment	A **fragment** is an incomplete piece of a sentence used by itself.
	◆ Perhaps not!
Full stop	The **full stop** indicates a definite pause. It is used at the end of all sentences that are not questions or exclamations.
	A sentence is a word or a group of words that makes complete sense on its own. Sentences begin with capital letters and end with full stops.
	◆ *My aunt took me to the zoo.*

Gender	Nouns can be male, female or neuter. Pronouns stand in ithe place of a noun, so they can also be male, female or neuter. To know the **gender** of a pronoun, look at the noun it stands for.

◆ The **boy** ran away. (male)

◆ **Sarah** laughed heartily. (female)

◆ The **rock** was very heavy. (neuter)

◆ **He** swam across the pool. (male pronoun)

Generic	A noun or noun phrase which denotes an entire class of things rather than one particular thing.

◆ dog, girl, happiness

◆ A cat is closely related to a tiger or lion.

Genre	**Genres** are the basic groups of writing. They include; recount, narrative, procedures, report, persuasive, explanation and verse.

Gerunds	A gerund is a form of verb containing verbal qualities but which may turn the entire verb phrase containing it into a noun phrase.

◆ **Flying** makes me nervous. (subject of the verb)

◆ One of his duties as head master was **attending** the parent meetings. (complement of the verb "to be."

◆ My brother-in-law is fond of **windsurfing**. (a gerund must come after a preposition.)

Homographs	Homographs are words that sound the same and are spelt the same, but have different meanings.

◆ *bear* (an animal), bear (to carry).

Homonyms	Homonyms are words that sound the same, but are spelt differently and have a different meaning.

◆ *right, write*

Homophones	**Homophones** are words that sound the same but have different meanings. They may be spelt differently. Homophones and homographs are both homonyms.

◆ son (child), sun (star)

◆ knot (tie with a rope), not (negative)

Hyphen	The **hyphen** may join several words into one word or divide a single word into separate parts.

◆ *pre-shrunk   free-for-all   make-believe*

A **hyphen** is used to join written compound numbers from twenty-one to ninety-nine.

◆ *twenty-five*   *fifty-two*   *eighty-seven*

A **hyphen** is used to join two parts of a written fraction.

◆ *two-thirds*

A **hyphen** is used to join the prefixes **ex-** and **self-** to a compound word.

◆ *ex-president*

A **hyphen** is used to join two or more words that combine into a compound adjective.

◆ *fancy-dress party*

Hyperbole

A **hyperbole** is an exaggeration aimed at making one's words more effective; but with no intention of deceiving.

◆ *I am so hungry I could eat a horse.*

Indefinite article

'**a**' is an indefinite article

◆ I am looking for **a** man to help. (Any man not a specific one.)

Indefinite pronoun

An **indefinite pronoun** is a pronoun that denotes nobody in particular.

◆ somebody, someone, something, anybody, anyone

Indirect speech

Indirect speech is reporting what someone says without quoting the exact words.

◆ Mary said that she'd love to come.

Irony

Irony is any gentle form of sarcasm in which the opposite of what is said is really meant.

◆ If there is something I cannot stand it is intolerance.

Metaphor

A **metaphor** is a simile taken one step farther.

◆ Instead of saying that *the pool is as clear as crystal*, we say *the crystal pool gleamed.*

A **metaphor** uses a word or words to suggest something different from their literal meaning.

◆ *a heart of stone.*

Monologue and soliloquy

A **monologue** is a long talk by one person.

A **soliloquy** is the act of talking when you are alone, or when you are pretending to be alone, as in a play.

Narrative	A **narrative** will tell a story. Not only will the details of the story follow in sequence but there will be a problem or complication to interest the reader. It will have a definite end. As well as telling who, what, why or where, it will contain: ◆ a setting ◆ a sequence of events including a problem ◆ a crisis ◆ an ending A **narrative** is a story with characters and a definite plot line. There are two types of narratives: fiction and non-fiction. A poem can also be a narrative.
Noun	A **noun** is the name of a person, place or thing. **Nouns** may be: 1. singular or plural 2. common or proper 3. masculine, feminine or neuter ◆ *John (male), Pamela, (female), rock (neuter)* 4. concrete or abstract 5. concrete nouns may be collective 6. they may be the subject or the object of the verb.
Noun - abstract	An **abstract noun** is the name of something that can exist in your mind although you can not see or hear it. ◆ *anger, beauty, despair, hope, greed, joy, kindness, sadness* ◆ *I cannot describe the <u>despair</u> I felt when I gazed on the remains of my house. (despair—**abstract noun**)* The kindness displayed by my neighbours after the fire enabled me to cope. (kindness - **abstract noun**)
Nouns -naming words	A **noun** names people, places or things.
Noun - common	**Common nouns** are the name of any common things. They do not have capital letters. ◆ *beach, tent*
Noun -collective	A **Collective noun** is a name given to a group of persons or things. ◆ *a <u>school</u> of fish.*

Noun -nominative	The **nominative noun** is the form of a noun or pronoun used in the subject. It comes in front of the verb. To find the noun in the nominative case, ask "who" or "what." ◆ *David went swimming.* ◆ Ask "who" went swimming? (David). Then David is in the nominative case.
Nouns in the nominative case	Sometimes two or more nouns can be in the nominative case in a sentence. ◆ *Both Jane and Mary came to tea.*
Nouns in apposition	Sometimes we use two titles, side by side, to refer to the same person. We call these nouns in apposition and they form the subject. ◆ *Mr. Jones, my swimming teacher, is on holiday.* ◆ *Mr. Jones, my swimming teacher* is the subject
Noun -possessive	**Possessive nouns** are used to show possession. They are words that would normally be nouns but are used as adjectives to modify a noun or pronoun. A possessive noun has an apostrophe. ◆ *Peter's screwdriver, sheep's wool.*
Nouns - proper	**Proper nouns** are the name of particular or specific people, places or things. ◆ *John, Australia, Melbourne Cricket Ground.*
Nouns - singular or plural	Singular means one. Plural means more than one. ◆ *one cat* (singular), *two cats* (plural).
Nouns - plural (f, fe)	With most words that end in **f** or **fe**, we drop the **f** and add **ves** to form the plural. ◆ *hoof, hooves*
Nouns - plural (o)	When nouns end in a consonant followed by an "**o**", add "**es**" to form the plural, for example, tomato becomes tomatoes. If the word is foreign and ends in "**o**", add "**s**" ◆ *photo becomes photos*
Nouns - Plurals (s)	We add "**s**" to most nouns to make them plural or more than one. ◆ *frog becomes frogs*

Nouns **- plurals (s, ss, sh,** **ch, x, or z)**	When a noun ends with **s, ss, sh, ch, x,** or **z**, add **es** to form the plural. ◆ *patch + es = patches*
Nouns **-plurals (y)**	If there is a vowel before the **y**, add **s** to form the plural, e ◆ *play becomes plays* Remember **y** can also be a vowel. If there is a consonant before the **y**, change **y** to **i** and add **es**. ◆ *daisy becomes daisies* Any kind of names ending in **y** takes **s** in the plural, even if there is no vowel before the **y** ◆ *Mr Murray or the Murrays.*
Nouns **- always plurals**	Some words, like cattle, are always plural.
Nouns **- plurals change** **spelling**	Some words change their spelling when they become plurals. ◆ *child* becomes *children.*
Nouns **- Plural spelling**	Some nouns are spelt the same if they are singular or plural. ◆ *deer* Some change completely. ◆ *mouse, mice*
Paragraph	A **paragraph** is a group of sentences about one topic. A **paragraph** is made up or two or more sentences.
Parentheses	**Parentheses**, also called **brackets**, are always used in pairs. They enclose extra information in the form of an example, a comment or an explanation. The bracket helps clarify or add to the information. Eat a green vegetable, (spinach, beans or peas) each day. Parentheses are also used to set off numbers or letters in an outline or list.
Participles	The **participle** is the form of the verb used in combination with an auxiliary verb, e.g., am, are ◆ *am walking*, to indicate tense, mood and voice.

Participle - present	A **present participle** is part of a verb that ends in "ing." These present participles are often used to begin phrases called participle phrases. ◆ *Jan is swimming well.* ◆ *Singing for joy, she danced across the kitchen.*
Participle - past	**Past participles** usually end in **ed** which is sometimes shortened to **t** or **d**. They are used with the helping verb "to have" to show the action has stopped. All past participles have helping verbs. Many strong verbs end in **n** or **en**, while others change altogether. A **past participle** indicates completed or past time. The past participle of a regular verb ends in **-ed**. Irregular verbs tend to end in **-en**. ◆ *wounded, painted, walked* -regular past participle ◆ *eat, ate, had eaten* - irregular past participle
Participle - past perfect	The **–ing** form of the verb <u>had</u> is combined with the past participle of the main verb. ◆ *Having finished dinner, he left the table.* *having* - past perfect *finished* - main verb
Participles that change	Some verbs change their spelling in the past tense and the past participle. These are strong verbs. ◆ *break* (infinitive) ◆ *broke* (past tense) ◆ *had broken* (past participle)
Personification	**Personification** is a type of metaphor. It gives human nature or form to something. ◆ *the <u>lonely</u> trees.*
Phrase	A **phrase** is a group of words that have no finite verb A phrase begins with a preposition. It adds to the meaning of the sentence. A phrase does not contain a subject or predicate. To identify the phrase first identify the subject and predicate. The phrase will begin with a preposition and contain no verb. A phrase cannot stand alone as a sentence. ◆ *The girl in the pretty dress is my sister.* *The girl is my sister,* The girl - subject *is my sister* - predicate *in the pretty dress* - phrase

Phrase - adjectival

An **adjectival phrase** functions like an adjective and can add meaning to a noun or pronoun. It may begin with a preposition or present or past participle.

- ◆ The boy <u>near me</u> was reading a book.
  near me - adjectival phrase
- ◆ The lady, <u>waiting near the stairs</u>, has just arrived.
  waiting near the stairs - adjectival phrase
- ◆ The chair <u>near the window </u>is comfortable.
  chair - noun, near the window - adjectival phrase as it adds to the knowledge of the chair.

Phrase - adverbial

An **adverbial phrase** adds meaning to a verb. They tell how, where, when or why.

- ◆ My friend always arrives <u>on time</u>. (on time tells when she arrives)

A phrase may begin with a preposition or an infinitive. An infinitive is the verb without any reference to the subject. It can not act as a complete verb in a sentence and is usually proceeded by "to."

- ◆ The girl ran <u>with great speed</u>. (with is the preposition)
- ◆ I beeped the horn <u>to startle the cat</u> that lay on the road. (infinitive)

Phrase - participle

A present participle is part of a verb that ends in "ing." These present participles are often used to begin phrases called **participle phrases.**

- ◆ *Singing for joy* - she danced across the kitchen.

Predicate

The **predicate** is the verb form in the subject that expresses the state or action of the subject. It includes the verb and all the words that follow.

Find the verb. The predicate follows it.

- ◆ James chased the cat.
  James is the subject, *chased the cat* is the predicate
- ◆ After the long day, Mary was glad to return home.
  Mary is the subject
  was glad to return home is the predicate

Prefix

A **prefix** comes at the beginning of a word and changes or adds to the meaning of the base word

- ◆ anti + septic (against germs) = antiseptic

You do not change the spelling of a word when adding a prefix, even when the last letter of the prefix is the same as the first letter of the word you are adding it to.

Example of prefixes are **pre-** and **re-**. The prefix **pre-** comes from Latin and means **before**.

The prefix **re-** comes from Latin and means **again, again and again, back or backwards**.

- *pre + school = preschool.*
- *re + cycle = recycle*

Persuasive essay or argument

The purpose of an **argumentative or persuasive essay** is to allow a person to present a point of view. It is organised into points to state a position. The argument backed up by evidence, a summing up and conclusion and finishes with a call for some action.

Prepositions

A preposition shows the relationship between nouns or pronouns and other words.

They are usually found in front of the noun or pronoun.

The most common prepositions are:

across	beneath	near	into	
over	after	to	between	
of	past	among	during	
like	up	around	from	
near	before	in	with	on

- *in the pool*
- *across the road*

Procedure

Procedure is a genre that describes how to do or make something. It will be organised into:

1. A statement of what is being made
2. A list of materials, equipment or ingredients needed.
3. Step by step instructions on what to do.
   (often these will be numbered.)

Pronoun

There are nine classes of **pronouns.**

1. **Personal**
First person pronouns are: **I, me, we, us.**
Second person pronouns are: **thou, thee, you.**
Third person pronouns are: **he, him, she, her, it, they, them.**

- He often comes to visit.

2. The **impersonal pronoun it** is used when it does not refer to any person or thing.
   - ◆ It is raining.

3. **relative**
   - ◆ The girl, who was very artistic, won the painting competition.

4. **interrogative**
   - ◆ Who is at the door?

5. **reflexive**
   - ◆ The young boy dressed himself.

6. **possessive**
   - ◆ The dog buried his bone.

7. **distributive**
   - ◆ Neither my brother nor I were tired.

8. **demonstrative**
   - ◆ I do not want this book.

9. **indefinite**
   - ◆ Everybody loves a day off.

Pronoun chart - singular

Person	Gender	Subject	Object	Reflective
1st	male/female	I	me	myself
2nd	male/female	you	you	yourself
3rd	male	he	him	himself
	female	she	her	herself
	neuter	it	it	itself

Pronoun chart - plural

Person	Gender	Subject	Object	Reflective
1st	male/female	we	us	ourselves
2nd	male/female	you	you	yourself
3rd	male/female/	they	them	themselves
	neuter	they	them	themselves

Pronouns - demonstrative

Demonstrative pronouns stand for and refer to a noun.

The demonstrative pronouns are: **that, this, those, these.**

- ◆ Those are my books.
  those - demonstrative pronoun, stands for the books.

If the **demonstrative pronoun** is followed by a noun, it becomes a **demonstrative adjective**.

- ◆ This hat is mine
  this - demonstrative   *hat* - describes which hat

Pronouns **- distributive**	**Distributive pronouns** point to separate things and therefore are always followed by a singular verb. ◆ *Each of you will stay in after school.* **N.B.** If the words are followed by a noun, they become distributive adjectives. ◆ *Each boy will stay after school.* Common forms are: **any**, **each, everyone, everybody, either, neither**.
Pronoun **- emphatic**	An **emphatic pronoun** emphasises a previously used noun. *She, **herself**, came. An emphatic pronoun is never used alone as the subject of a verb.*
Pronoun **- indefinite**	**Indefinite pronouns** are pronouns which replace nouns without specifying which noun they replace. **anybody, everybody, everything, all, most, many, several.** They usually end in **-body**, **-one**, or **-thing**. If they end in **-body,** or **-one**, e.g., *anybody, anyone*, they will be common gender. If they end in **-thing e.g.,** *anything*, they will be neuter gender. ◆ *Does anybody want to come with me?*
Pronoun **- interrogative**	**Interrogative pronouns** are used to ask questions. The interrogative pronouns are: **who, whom, whose, which, what** ◆ *Whose hat is this?* (**whose**, an interrogative pronoun, relates to the hat.)
Pronoun **- personal**	A **Personal Pronoun** is used in place of a person or thing. **I, he, she, we, you, they, me, her, him, it, us, you, them.** Nouns and pronouns display case according to their function in the sentence. They can be subjective, nominative or possessive or objective.
Pronoun **- possessive**	A **Possessive Pronoun** is a word that is used in place of a noun. ◆ <u>*she*</u> *instead of Mary* A **Possessive Pronoun** stands in place of a noun and shows ownership. **Mine, yours, his, hers, its, ours, your, theirs** are all possessive pronouns.

Pronoun - reflexive	A **reflexive pronoun** refers back to the subject of the sentence. Examples are **myself, himself, ourselves, themselves, itself.** ◆ *Don hurt <u>himself</u> on the nail.*
Pronoun - relative	**Relative pronouns** relate to a noun or personal pronoun. The relative pronoun has to agree in number. Some relative pronouns are **who, whom, whose, which, that.** ◆ *Peter, whom I have known for a long time, has won first prize in his course.* (**whom**, a relative pronoun, relates to Peter.)
Proverbs	**Proverbs** are wise sayings that teach us basic truths. They are often metaphorical rather than literal. A metaphor is a figure of speech in which something is spoken of as if it was something else. ◆ *Don't count your chickens before they are hatched.* (This has nothing to do with chickens, it means don't count or spend something until you have it.)
Pun	A **pun** is a play on words.
Punctuation	**Punctuation** makes it easier to read information.
Onomatopoeia	**Onomatopoeia** is the name given to a word when the word has the same meaning as its sound. ◆ *crash, bang, buzz*
Question marks	A **question mark** is used at the end of a sentence that asks a question. ◆ *How are you?*
Quotation marks or inverted commas	**Quotation marks** (speaking marks) tell us what is said. ◆ *"How are you today?" asked John.* Sometimes quotation marks are in two different parts of the sentence. ◆ *"I am going to the shops, " said Mother. "Do you want to come with me?*
Recount	In a recount the writer puts down his or her experiences. These may be personal events, factual incidents or imaginary events. It will tell about "who, what and where" the incident occurred. The sequence of events will be written in order.

| **Reflexive Pronoun** | A **reflexive pronoun** refers back to the subject of the sentence. |

Examples are **myself, himself, ourselves, themselves, itself**.

◆ *Don hurt himself on the nail.*

Rhetorical Question

A **rhetorical question** is a question that is asked merely for effect and which does not expect an answer.

◆ Do you see what I mean?

| **Report** | The purpose of a **report** is to give facts and information about a topic. It does not answer the questions why or how. |

It is organised into a generalised statement about the nature of the report and facts about the subject are set out in paragraphs.

Semicolon

A **semicolon** is not half a colon. It is a punctuation mark stronger than a comma but less than a full stop. use a semi-colon when a full stop is possible but would separate the sentences too strongly.

◆ I said it would rain today; I was right.

A **semi-colon** may be used before such words and expressions as **nevertheless, therefore, however, instead, yet, for example** and **consequently**.

◆ He was the eldest son; consequently he inherited the title.

A **semi-colon** may be used to separate items on a list.

◆ Important food groups include: milk, butter and cheese; meat, poultry and eggs; green or yellow vegetables; cereals.

Sentences

Sentences must contain a noun (or pronoun) and a verb. A sentence always begins with a capital letter and ends with a full stop.

There are six kinds of sentences.

1. Statements

◆ *It is raining.* - communicating an observation

◆ *It may rain.* - communicating an inference

◆ *This is the heaviest rain this year.* - communicating reasoning

2. Questions

- *Did you see that?* - electing a direct answer
- *Should I do that?* - expressing doubt
- *Who could be so stupid as to do that?* - a rhetorical question not requiring an answer.

3. Commands

- *Stop it!* - requiring direct action
- *Help me!* - invite a decision to act

4. Exclamations

- *What a mess.* - expressing feelings in a direct way

5. Greetings

- *Good morning* - a conversational greeting not in the form of a statement or question.

6. Responses

- *I agree* - a response to what has been said

Sentences - simple

A **simple sentence** has a subject and predicate.

- *John ran.*
  John (subject), *ran* (verb - predicate)

- *Help me!*
  you (subject - understood), *help* (verb - predicate)

Sentences - complex

A **complex sentence** contains a principal and sub-ordinate clause.

- *I ate the meal that you cooked.*
  I ate the meal (principal clause.)
  that you cooked (sub-ordinate clause

Sentence Type

Sentences can be classified by their grammatical form: **declarative, interrogative, imperative, exclamatory (or statement, question, command** and **exclamation.)**

- It is a wet day. (declarative)
- Are you coming to the shops with me? (interrogative)
- Put the books on the table right now please. (imperative)
- What a nuisance! (exclamatory)

Simile

A **simile** asks us to picture one thing as being similar to another and uses the words "like" or "as," to create the comparison in our minds.

- *as slippery as an eel*

A **metaphor** is a simile taken one step farther. For example instead of saying that the pool is as clear as crystal, we say the pool is crystal.

Soliloquy and monologue

A **soliloquy** is the act of talking when you are alone, or when you are pretending to be alone, as in a play.

A **monologue** is a long talk by one person.

Spoonerism

A **spoonerism** occurs when we accidently change the position of letters in words so what is meant to be serious sounds ridiculous.

◆ a lack of pies   (a pack of lies)

Statement

A **statement** is a sentence that states a fact. It has a clear meaning and expresses a clear thought, e.g., It rained during the evening.

Subject and predicate

Every sentence is made up of two parts: the **Subject**, which is the part of the sentence about which something is being said; and the **Predicate**, which makes a statement about the Subject.

The keyword of the Subject is always a **noun**.

The keyword of the Predicate is always a **verb**.

◆ *The old lady smiled. lady* - subject; *smiled* - predicate.

The subject does not always appear before the verb.

◆ *On the hill stands a lighthouse.*
verb - *stands*.
What stands? - *a lighthouse. a lighthouse* is the subject.

◆ In the sentence, "Here is your hat," finding the subject can be tricky. Ask yourself "here is what?"
The answer is the subject - your hat, *is here* is the predicate.

Subordinate Clause

A **subordinate clause** adds meaning to a principal clause.

◆ When the rain ceased we hurried home.
we hurried home - principal clause
When the rain ceased - subordinate clause

Subordinating Conjunction

A **subordinating conjunction** is the part of speech containing the words which can introduce an adverbial clause. These include **after, although, as, if, because, before, even if, in order that, once, provided that, rather than, since, so that, than. that, though, unless, until, when, whenever, whether, while** and **why.**

- ◆ Jim will wash the dishes once Mary has finished her dinner.
- ◆ We looked on top of the refrigerator because Frank would often leave his wallet there.

Superlative

The **superlative** is form of the adjective or adverb expressing the highest degree.

The **positive** is the basic form of the adjective.

The **comparative** is the form of the adjective that is constructed with 'er' or with more.

- ◆ big (positive),   bigger (comparative), biggest (superlative)
- ◆ good (positive) better (comparative) best (superlative)

Suffix

A **suffix** is a word or syllable added at the end of the word to change or add to its meaning.

- ◆ *forget + ful*

When adding an ending (suffix) to a **silent e**, drop the e when the suffix you are adding begins with a vowel.

- ◆ *hope* becomes *hoping*.

When a word ends in **ie**, change the word to **y** before adding **–ing.**

- ◆ *die + ing = dying.*

-age is a suffix. It comes from Latin and changes the word to a noun. It has several meanings including:

- ◆ *sewage, an amount*
- ◆ *footage, an action*
- ◆ *breakage, a condition or state*
- ◆ *vicarage, a residence*

The suffix **-ment** changes the word to a noun. It shows an action,

- ◆ *appeasement, the result of an action*
- ◆ *advancement, or the means or process of an action*

Keep the **e** when: a word ends in **ge** or **ce**; when adding a suffix beginning with **–able** or **–ous**, keep the **e** to prevent confusion.

- ◆ notice + able = noticeable
- ◆ *dye + ing becomes dyeing (not dying)*

Keep the **e** when the endings **ye, oe** and **ee** come before the suffix.

◆ *canoe + ing = canoeing*

When adding a suffix to a word ending in **y**, if there is a consonant before the **y**, change the **y** to **i** and add the suffix.

◆ *marry + ed = married*

When adding a suffix to a word ending in **y**, if the suffix begins with an **i** keep the **y**.

◆ *study + ing = studying*

When adding a suffix to a word ending in **y**, change the **y** to **ie** when you add an **s**.

◆ *beauty + s = beauties*

Syllables

A **syllable** is the part of the word which is spoken by a single impulse of the voice. Every part of the syllable must contain a vowel.

◆ in/vite, tel/e/phone, sim/ple, re/li/able

Divide a **compound word**, e.g., **bathrobe**, between the words that form the compound word

◆ *bath/ robe.*

Syllables & vowels

When a **vowel** is sounded alone in a word it forms a syllable by itself.

◆ *e/ven*

Verbs

A verb is any word or group of words that express what action has, is or will take place.

Verbs may be **singular or plural**

◆ John **is** present today. (singular)
We **are** all present today. (plural)

◆ The number of boys in the class is now fifty.(
the number—singular

◆ A number of glasses have been taken.
a number of (several) - plural

Verb agreement

The verb must agree in person and number with its subject. If the **subject** is singular the verb must be singular. If the subject is plural, the verb must be plural.

◆ *The cake looks very nice.*
(The cake is the subject. Looks is the singular verb)

◆ *The cakes look nice.*
(The cakes is the subject. Look is the plural verb.)

Verb agreement	The following words always have a singular verb: anybody, everybody, nobody, anyone, everyone, no one, none.

◆ *Everybody wants to attend the concert tomorrow.*
(Everybody is the subject. Wants is the singular verb.)

Verb - finite	A **finite verb** is a verb that has a subject. The verb must agree with its subject in person and number, e.g., The boy ran fast.

Verb - infinitive	The **infinitive** is the verb without any reference to the subject. It can not act as a complete verb in a sentence. It is often preceded by the word "to".

◆ I sounded the horn **to startle** the cat that sat on the road.

Verb -intransitive	An **intransitive verb** has no object.

◆ The baby is still crying.

Verb -non finite	A **non-finite verb** can not stand alone without the help of an auxiliary verb.

◆ The boy <u>was running</u> fast.

Verb number

The **verb number** refers to whether the verb is singular or plural. If the subject is plural the verb must be plural.

◆ The boy   runs   down the streets.
   (singular subject)   (singular verb)

◆ The boys   run   down the street
   (plural subject)   (plural verb)

**Verbs
Regular and
Irregular verbs**

Most **regular verbs** form their tenses in the same way.

present   jump
past   jumped
future   will jump

Some **irregular verbs** change their spelling in the past tense and past participle.

◆ do, did, done

The most common **irregular verbs** are:

Present	Past	Past Participle
arise	arose	arisen
be	was/were	been
become	became	become
drink	drank	drunk

drink	drank	drunk
choose	chose	chosen
draw	drew	drawn
eat	ate	eaten
fly	flew	flown
get	got	got
give	gave	given
go	went	gone
know	knew	known
lend	lent	lent
lie	lay	lain
ring	rang	rung
see	saw	seen
speak	spoke	spoken
take	took	taken
wear	wore	worn
write	wrote	written

N.B. Past participles are preceded by part of another verb, usually the verb have.

◆ I fly to Adelaide regularly.

◆ I flew to Adelaide. (past tense)

◆ I have flown to Adelaide. (past participle)

Verb tense

The **verb tense** refers to when the action is happening: present, past or future.

◆ Bob helps Mum. (present tense)

◆ Bob helped Mum yesterday. (past tense)

◆ Bob will help Mum tomorrow. (future tense)

Verb -transitive

A **transitive verb** has an object. To find the object of a sentence, ask who or what after the verb. If there is no object, the verb is non-transitive.

◆ John ran behind the car. Ran is the finite verb. John is the subject. The car is the object so the verb is transitive.

Remember to find the object, ask "who?" or "what?" after the verb.

Spelling Rules

Anagrams

Anagrams are words that have had their letters rearranged to make a new word with no letters missing and no letters addd.

◆ horse, shore; care, race.

Antonyms

Antonyms are words that have the opposite meaning.

◆ *the opposite of vigilant is heedless.*

a:

a is sounded as the short **o** after **qu**, **w** and **wh**

◆ squash. was, what

a:

The **ah** sound of the letter **a**, as in father, is usually followed by two consonants.

◆ dart, bath.

ay:

We use **ay** at the end of a word, but we never use **ai** at the end of a word.

◆ say not sai.

c:

When **c** is followed by **e**, **i** or **y** it often makes the **s** sound.

◆ cent, police, cycle

The most **commonly confused words** are:

s	c	sc
apprehensive	competence	abscess
defence	adolescent	resuscitate
evidence	convalescent	luscious
license (verb)	licence (noun)	omniscient
offence	iridescent	
practise (verb)	practice (noun)	
pretence	conscience	
deficient	conscious	
malicious	crescent	
suspicious		

c and k:

c and **k** both make the same sound. The **k** sound is written **c** before **a**, **o** and **u**.

◆ cat, cot, cut.

The **k** sound is written **k** before **e** and **i**.

◆ kill, kick, kitten

Words like kangaroo have been taken from other languages

ck:	**ck** is used only after a short vowel.
	◆ sock
	It is never used at the beginning of a word. If another consonant follows the **k** sound, the letter **k** is not needed.
	◆ act

| **-cian:** | **-cian** is used mostly for people. |
| | ◆ electrician, musician, politician |

| **Compound words** | Compound words are two base words joined together to form a single word, |
| | ◆ bushranger, iceberg, jigsaw |

| **Consonants** | b, c, d, f, g, h, j, k, l, m, n, p, q, r, s, t, v, w, x, y, z |

| **Contractions** | **Contractions** are two words that have been shortened to one. |
| | ◆ aren't instead of are not |

dge:	**dge** is used only after a short vowel.
	◆ bridge, fudge
	We add **d** to make the vowel short. If we only had the **ge**, the vowel would be long.
	◆ cage

Doubling Rule	We usually double **f, l, s** and **z** in short words (one syllable) after a short vowel which says **a, e, i, o, u**.
	◆ fluff, bell, fuss, buzz.
	We double **b, d, g, l, m, n, p** and **t** only when they follow a short vowel and we add an ending beginning with a vowel. (vowel + consonant + vowel),
	◆ hop + p + ed hot + t + er

| **e:** | **e** at the end of a word makes the previous vowel long (say its own name). |
| | ◆ **a** in **cake**,   **e** as in **these**, **i** as in **vine**, **o as in bone**,   **u** as in tube. |

e:	When words end in an **e,** the final **e** is retained when a suffix beginning with a consonant is added.

◆ genuine + ly = genuinely

e:	When adding an ending (suffix) to a silent **e,** drop the **e** when the suffix you are adding begins with a vowel.

◆ hope + ing = hoping

e:	**e** often follows **v** at the end of a word since **v** can never be used at the end of an English word.

◆ love, pave

ea:	**ea** is a vowel diagraph. If one syllable has two vowels, the first is usually long and the second is usually silent.

◆ seal, weak, tease

Two vowels found together are not always vowel diagraphs. Sometimes vowels are separated by syllables and pronounced separately.

◆ acreage (acre/age) changeable (change/able)

f:	When a word ends with an **f** sound, as in knife, we can not just add **s** to make it plural (more than one). Instead we drop the **f** and add **v** (e).

◆ knives, shelves

g:	When **g** is followed by **e, i** or **y** it will often have the **j** sound.

◆ germ, gypsy

Greek Prefixes Examples

Word	Meaning	Derived words
amphi-	both, about	amphibious
ana-	up, back, again	anagram, anachronism
auto-	self	automatic, automobile
cata-	downwards	catastrophic
deca-	ten	December, decimal
di-	two	dichloride, divide
dia-	through	diagram, dialogue
dis-	two	dissect
ex-	out	exodus, excavate
en-	in	energy, encamp, encase

Word	Meaning	Derived words
epi-	in	epidemic, epidermis
eu-	well, good	eucalypt, eugenic
hemi-	half	hemisphere
hexa-	six	hexagonal, hexameter
homo-	the same	homogeneous, homonym
hyper-	above, excessive	hypercritical, hyperactive
hypo-	under, slight	hypodermic, hypocrite
mega-	great	megalomaniac
mono-	one	monogamous, monologue
para-	beside, against	parallel, parasite, paragraph
penta-	five	pentagon, pentathlon
peri-	round about	periscope, perimeter
proto-	first	prototype, protoplasm
pro-	before	prophet, programme
syn-	with	synthetic, synthesize
tri-	three	tricycle, trigonometry

Homographs

Homographs are words that both sound the same and are written the same but have different meanings.

- ◆ to show (verb)   a show (noun).

Homonym

Homonym is the general name given to words that sound the same but are spelt differently and have different meanings,

- ◆ aren't, aunt

or words that are spelt the same way as another word but have a different meaning.

- ◆ novel (story)   novel (different)

Homophones and **homographs** are both **homonyms**.

Homophones

Homophones are words that sound the same, but are spelt differently.

- ◆ knight, night.

i:

i often says the long vowel sound before 2 consonants.

- ◆ mind, grind.

i:	**i** before **e** except after **c** but only when it says **ee**,	
	◆ receive not relieve,	
i, j, u, v:	are never used at the end of an English word. Words with **i** at the end are taken from another language.	
	◆ The word "ski" comes from Norway.	
	◆ Taxi is a shortened word, (taximeter).	
ie:	When a word ends in **ie**, to make it plural change the i**e** to **y** before adding **–ing**.	
	◆ die becomes dying	
igh:	**igh** says the long **i** sound. The **gh** is silent.	
	◆ night, fright, high	
j:	We can not use **j** at the end of an English word.	
k:	The **k** sound before **t** in **–tion** is always spelt **c**.	
	◆ action	
kn:	**kn** is only used at the beginning of a word and never in the middle or end of a word.	
	◆ knee, knock	
	When a **kn** word ends in f, such as knife, we can not just add **s** to make it plural. Instead we drop the **f** and add **v** (e).	
	◆ knife, knives	

Latin Roots Examples

Many of our words derive from Latin. The Latin root gives us a clue to the meaning of the word.

Word	Meaning	Derived words
alter	other	alteration, alternative
audio	I hear	audience, audition
annus	year	annual, anniversary
biblion	book	Bible, bibliography
capio	I sieze	capture, captive
clausus	I shut	exclude, include, close, enclose, conclude
credo	I believe	credible, credit
centum	hundred	century, percent
equus	horse	equestrian, equine

Word	Meaning	Derived words
finis	the end	final, finish, finalize
geo	earth	geology, geography
jevunus	young	juvenile, rejuvenate
magnus	great	magnify, magnitude, magnificent
mater	mother	maternal, maternity
mikros	small	microscope, microbe
navis	ship	navy, navigate
oculus	eye	binoculars
pater	father	paternal, paternity
populus	people	population, metropolitan
primus	first	premier, primitive, primary
rectus	I rule	correct, direct, regulate
scriptum	I write	scripture, script, transcribe
terra	the earth	terrace, territory

m and n: When we double **m** or **n**, we often write **el** to complete the syllable,

- ◆ tunnel, pommel

ng: The **ng** sound comes only after a short vowel that says **a**, **e**, **i**, **o**, **u**,

- ◆ hang, bang, sung

or: **or** makes the **er** sound when it follows **w**.

- ◆ worm.

oy: We use **oy** at the end of a word, but we never use **oi** at the end of a word

- ◆ boy not boi

Plurals We add **s** to most nouns to make them plural or more than one.

- ◆ <u>frog</u> becomes <u>frogs</u>

When a noun ends with **s, ss, sh, ch** (as in chicken), **x** or **z** add **es** to form the plural.

- ◆ patch + es = patches

Plurals

When changing words ending in **y** to form a plural. If there is a vowel before the **y**, just add **s** to form the plural.

◆ alley + s = alleys

If there is a consonant before the **y**, change the **y** to **i** and add **es**,

◆ *melody* becomes *melodies*

Any kind of name ending in **y** takes **s** in the plural, even if there is a consonant before the **y**.

◆ Mr *Murray* or the *Murrays* (the family)

Words ending in **f**, **fe** or **ff**: Most words drop the **f** or **fe** and add **ves** to make the word plural.

◆ *leaf* becomes *leaves*

A few words add **s** to form the plural.

◆ *chief* becomes *chiefs*

When nouns end in **o**:

If a noun ends in a consonant followed by **o**, add **es** to form the plural.

◆ *tomato* becomes *tomatoes*

If words have a foreign origin and end in **o**, add **s**

◆ *photos*

Prefixes

A prefix comes at the beginning of a word and changes or adds to the meaning of the base word.

◆ anti + septic (against germs) = antiseptic

You do not change the spelling of a word when adding a prefix, even when the last letter of the prefix is the same as the first letter of the word you are adding it to.

◆ dis + solve = dissolve   mis + spell = misspell

Prefix-examples:

ab–	away from
ac–	to, towards, at or about. It is used instead of
ad–	used before c and qu: to, towards, next to
anthropo–	human being
biblio–	book
bio–	life or living things
con–	before

Prefix-examples		
de–	means remove, away, down, reversal	
dis–	inability, reversal, removal or lack	
in–, im–	not	
ir–	not	
mis–	wrong	
pre–	before, in advance of, in front of	
re–	again	
se–	aside or apart	
sub–	under	
trans–	across	
un–	not	

q: **q** is never seen without **u**. (QANTAS is not a word. It stands for Queensland and Northern Territory Aerial Service.)

◆ queen, quick

s: **s** never says **z** at the beginning of a word. Instead we use **z** as in zebra.

sc: **sc** says **s** when followed by **e, i** or **y,**

◆ scene, science, scythe

sh: **sh** comes at the beginning of the word or the end of a syllable.

ship, dash

- sion: is used if the base word ends in **de, se** or **s,**

◆ provide becomes provision,

◆ revise becomes revision,

◆ confess becomes confession.

Suffixes

Suffixes usually change the parts of speech of the original word or root. They do this in several ways.

When adding an ending (suffix) to a silent **e**, drop the **e** when the suffix you are adding begins with a vowel.

◆ *hope becomes hoping*

They can indicate a doer (ard, art, er, ar, or, ier, yer, ster)

◆ doct**or**, bak**er**, glaz**ier**, lawy**er**, spinst**er**.

© Valerie Marett and Carmel Musumeci
Coroneos Publications

Australian Homeschooling #567
English Handbook

They can show a place. (ery, ry, y, stead)

- bak**ery**, pharmac**y**, home**stead**

They can give the general idea of a condition or state of
something or someone.
(craft, dom, fare, hood, ness, lock, red, ship, th)

- handi**craft**, wis**dom**, wel**fare**, boy**hood**, wed**lock**,
  knowledge, witness, hatred, length.

They can change the word to an abstract noun.

- justice, homage, arrogance

They can change words into action verbs. (en, er, se, le)

- short**en**, incen**se**, glitt**er**, prat**tle**

They can change the word to an adjective.
(en, ern, ward, wards, ey, y, ful, ish, ly, some, less, al)

- legal, woollen, backwards, dirty, fearful, foolish, lifelike,
  kindly, quarrelsome, fearless.

They can change the word to an adverb. (ly, long, wise)

- slowly, sidelong, otherwise

They can indicate a plural. (en)

- ox, oxen

Some suffixes make things and people smaller.
(en, y, ey, ie, kin, let, et, ling, ock)

- maid**en**, mumm**y**, pump**kin**, lock**et**, duck**ling**, bull**ock**

**Suffixes
- changing**

They can change words into action verbs. (en, er, se, le)

- short**en**, incen**se**, glitt**er**, prat**tle**.

Keep the **e** when a word ends in **ge** or **ce** when adding a
suffix beginning with **–able** or **–ous.**

- notice + able = noticeable

- manage + able = manageable

To prevent confusion.

- *dye + ing becomes dyeing (not dying)*

When the endings **ye**, **oe** and **ee** come before the suffix.

- canoe + ing = canoeing

When a word ends in **ie**, change the word to **y** before
adding **–ing.**

- *die + ing = dying*

**Suffixes
- changing**

When adding a suffix to a word ending **y** if there is a consonant before the **y**, change the **y** to **i** and add the suffix.

◆ <u>marry + ed</u> = <u>married</u>

If the suffix begins with an **i** keep the **y**.

◆ *<u>study + ing</u> = <u>studying</u>*

Change the **y** to **ie** when you add an **s**.

◆ *<u>beauty + s</u> = <u>beauties</u>*

Words that have only one syllable usually keep the **y** except before **es** and **ed**.

◆ <u>fly + er</u> = <u>flyer</u>

◆ <u>dry + ed</u> = <u>dried</u>

**Suffixes
- Examples**

–able	capable of; able to
–ance, **–ancy**	forms a noun expressing a quality or state, e.g.,arrogance or an action, e.g., assistance.
–ary	one who
–ate	forms nouns; condition of, the office of, the estate of
–ean	living in: European
–ent, **–ant**	having the quality of or incumbent, stringent, performing the action of, dormant
–ian	belonging to; Grecian
–ible	having the character or quality of audible
–ious	forms an adjective; having the qualities of; full of
–ise	to cause to become
–less	lacking or without; not susceptible to or capable of being; lifeless; stainless
–ly	being or acting as; in a certain way; friendly; quickly; manner of time; with respect to recently
–ment	a resulting state, action or process
–ness	**is** used to form nouns from adjectives and participles and means quality or state.

Suffix
- Examples

–ous   state or condition; having the quality of; it turns the word into an adjective.

–sion   act, process or state of.

–tion   changes a verb into a noun.

Syllable   A syllable is a letter or group of letters in which one vowel sound is heard.

◆   won/der/ful   (3 syllables)

◆   o/pen   (2 syllables

tch: is used only after a short vowel.

◆   batch.

The exceptions are such, which, rich and sandwich.

–tion: **—tion** is more commonly used than **–sion**. If the base word ends with **t** or **te**, then **–tion** will be used,

◆   act becomes action,

◆   complete becomes completion.

–tion is generally used for things.

u: English words do not end in **u**—exception "you".

v: **e** often follows **v** at the end of a word.

◆   live

v can never be at the end of an English word.

um: If a word ends in **um**, the word is generally derived from Latin.

◆   memorandum

To change a Latin word ending in **um** to plural, drop the **um** and add **a**.

◆   memoranda

wh: **wh** says **hw** as in what. We only say the first sound. In other **wh** words, the **w** is silent,

◆   whom

y: In English every syllable must have a vowel. **y** is often used when there is no other vowel. It makes the long **i** sound,

◆   shy, fly.

y: If **y** comes at the beginning of a word or syllable, it is a consonant,

◆ yo-yo, yoghurt

y: If **y** is the only vowel at the end of a word of more than one syllable it has a long **e** sound,

◆ berry, icy

y: When a word ends in **y** and you add a suffix beginning with **i**, keep the **y**,

◆ supply, supplying

y: If **y** is the only vowel at the end of a word of more than one syllable, it has the long **e** sound,

◆ baby, marry.

y: If a word ends in **y** and there is a consonant before the **y**, we change the **y** to **i** and add **es.**

◆ cherry, cherries.

Writing Rules

Advertisements: Understanding Terms Used

The purpose of an advertisement is to sell you (the consumer) a product, which, before you saw the advertisement, you may not have known you wanted or needed. For example, most families are quite happy with their current computer games until publicity is released about a new series of games.

You will find some of the terms commonly used in advertisements explained below.

Free!   Bonus

Nothing is ever free. The business has included the cost of their "give away" in the price you are paying. The word "free" is intended to make the purchase more acceptable and attractive to the buyer.

Special Offer   Limited Offer

These advertisements are intended to make the purchaser buy immediately. They convey the idea that the offer is for a limited time and if not purchased immediately, the purchaser may miss out. The purchaser needs to ask themselves why the item is on special; why the offer is limited; do they really need the item; can they afford it; and is there really an advantage in purchasing it now?

Discount   Discounted Price

Discounts are often genuine, for example, clothing discounts at the end of the season. In clothing stores the proprietor may wish to get rid of clothes left from the current season, which he will not be able to sell next season, and free up cash to purchase new stock.

In other cases, for example electrical retail stores, the item being discounted may be a superseded model, with a new model about to be released. Or alternatively the store may have imported a limited amount of stock for the sale. If the item is needed this may be a good time to purchase it.

Cash Back $800 off

"Cash Back" is usually an incentive on the part of the manufacturer to encourage a customer to purchase their product rather than a competitor's. To obtain cash back on a purchase, a purchaser usually has to pay the full price and then send a voucher, signed by the distributor, with a copy of the receipt to the manufacturer and wait a period of time for the manufacturer to refund the money.

However when an advertisement offers "Cash Off or "$'s Off" it is important to read the advertisement carefully. Generally the price shown is the price you will pay. The cash has already been deducted. The item being offered may be a superseded model or a model purchased specially for the sale.

Lowest Price Guaranteed   Guarantee

These terms are not the same. A guarantee is a warranty by a manufacturer, generally under certain conditions and for a specific length of time. These terms and conditions need to be read carefully. In simple terms, a guarantee states that the manufacturer is sure he is selling a good product and will promise to either fix it or replace it should the purchaser encounter problems due to faulty manufacture.

When an advertisement says that the lowest price is guaranteed the distributor will often match a competitors' price if it is lower and the purchaser can prove it. This is optional. The distributor is not really guaranteeing anything, just trying to encourage a purchase.

Advertisements sometimes state that satisfaction is guaranteed or your money will be refunded, generally within 30 days. Legally a business is required to refund money if a customer has been unable to view the product before purchasing, e.g., they bought it from an advertisement on TV, and if the product is not suitable for the purpose for which it was purchased. A customer is not entitled to a refund simply because they change their mind.

In some states the law safeguards the purchaser if they change their mind after they have purchased the item from a door to door salesman. This is called a "cooling off period" and is usually only a couple of days.

From

This is generally written in small print. It indicates that prices begin at a certain level. The picture shown in the advertisement may or may not be the price advertised.

Win!

The advertisement generally encourages the purchaser to buy a product to have a chance of winning a prize. There will be very few prizes compared to the number of purchasers so the chance of winning are slim.

Buy Now! Pay Later!   No Interest for 2 Years

The intention of the advertiser is to sell their product. The advertisement entices the buyer with the idea that even if they can not afford it now, it does not matter. They have time to pay for it.

The shop has actually arranged a loan for the purchaser. The loan generally requires minimum payments. These minimum payments do not usually clear the loan within the time period. If the loan is not totally paid in the period allotted, the interest for the whole period becomes due. This may be as high as 20%. Often a type of credit card will be given to the purchaser and statements will be sent out each month. By law, each statement must include how long the loan will take to repay if only the minimum payment is made.

The following might appear on an interest free loan of $2,200 over 2 years for a coffee machine:

If you make only the minimum payment & make no additional charges each month you pay	You will pay off the closing balance shown on this statement in about…	And you will end up paying an estimated total of interest charges of ……..
Only minimum payment	10 years and 7 months	$1,935.66
$96.00	2 years	$25.76

Note the small print. The rest of the bill will be in a much larger print.

The company that has lent the money does not really expect or want the purchaser to pay the total amount before the end of the interest free period. To take advantage of this offer, a purchaser needs to be disciplined in their repayments. The intention of the advertiser is to sell their product. The advertisement entices the buyer with the idea that even if they can not afford it now, it does not matter as they have time to pay for it.

If paid off within the time allowed it can be a great way of funding essential white goods, e.g., washing machine or refrigerator providing there is room in the budget for these monthly repayments.

Seeing the method of payment is via a credit card, once the item has been paid for the card should be put away safely and not used again.

A Book Report

1. **Choose between fiction and non-fiction, that is a story or a factual book.** It is important to choose the type of book you like or you will not write a good book report.

2. **Choose and read the book.** Find somewhere quiet where you are unlikely to be disturbed. Take your time reading the book. You should read the book from cover to cover at least once. This should be enjoyable and not a chore. Never make any notes in the book or high-light the facts. Write any notes or comments in an exercise book.

3. **As you read each chapter take notes.** You will want to note the following:

Fiction books:

a. setting of the book:
   - where the story takes place (where)
   - time, including the time of day and the period (when)
   - how the place appears or how the person arrived; it may also include the weather, plants and animals, means of transport etc. (how)

b. Period of time it is set in.

c. Each character as they appear: a brief description of their appearance and the part they play.

d. The main character or characters you will need to follow from chapter to chapter as their actions change.

Non-fiction books:

a. subject—a sentence or two on the general subject.

b. summary— a summary of what the author has to say about the subject. Note only the main points.

4. **When you have read the book at least once, fill out either the sheet provided for fiction or non-fiction on the next two pages.** This will help you clarify your thoughts before writing the book report.

5. **Write a rough draft using the summary you have made on the form.. Conclude the report by expressing your thoughts about what you have read.** Explain why the author wrote the book and what interested you most and what you have learnt.

6. **Correct your work.** You will find a checklist in this book. Sentence structure and paragraphing are important.

Book Report — Fiction

Follow steps 1 and 2 of the Book Report. Use the form
below to make notes for the outline for your report.

Title and Author: _____

Time Period: _____

Setting: _____
_____
_____
_____
_____
_____

Main Character or Characters:
_____
_____
_____
_____
_____
_____

Conclusion:
_____
_____
_____
_____
_____

Main Events: _____
_____
_____
_____
_____
_____
_____
_____

The Plot: _____
_____
_____
_____
_____
_____

Book Report — Non-Fiction

Follow steps 1 and 2 of the Book Report. Use the form below to make notes for the outline for your report.

Title and Author: _____

Subject: the type of information the book is about.

_____

_____

_____

_____

Summary: the facts or what the author had to say about the subject.

_____

_____

_____

_____

_____

_____

Conclusion: impressions of the book. Did you enjoy it?

_____

_____

_____

Critical Thinking

This is considered to be the "Information Age." More information is available on many subjects than has ever been available before, but is it all really "information?" Information is defined in a dictionary as "knowledge given or received concerning some fact or circumstances." A lot of the "information" we receive today is **opinion, gossip** or **propaganda**, which may or may not contain some factual basis.

Ask yourself therefore, when reading information from places like social networking sites, encyclopaedias, government sites, newspapers, emails and websites whether it is opinion, gossip, propaganda or facts.

We can see then that information we receive is not always factual. We need to take time to consider carefully most information, unless we are using resources such as an encyclopaedia, text book, or a government website such as Scam Watch. Text books may also include the author's conclusion on a theory or situation in history. Providing these are based on fact there is no reason to doubt them, although it does not hurt to consider other interpretations before making up your mind.

There is great power in spoken or written words. Words are powerful instruments that can be used to sway, persuade or hurt people.

Consider these quotations:

- The pen is mightier than the sword. *Edward Bulwer—Lytton*

- Speech is the mirror of the soul; as a man speaks, so is he. *Publius Syrus*

- Handle them carefully, for words have more power than an atom bomb. *Pearl Strachan*

- The flood of careless, unconsidered, cheap words is the greatest enemy of the profound word. *Stephen L Talbot*

Words are used every day on television, in the newspaper, on the internet, in magazines and many other places to persuade us to think a particular way or follow a particular course of action.

For example: The government now refers to people as "human resources." When we consider what this means, certain thoughts spring to mind, a few of which are outlined below.

- resources are usually a source of income

- resources are often exploited

- to consider people as human resources is to place little value on them individually as people

Politicians use words to convince you that their ideas and methods are correct and they are worthy of your vote. Words are generally chosen carefully to sway your opinion in favour of them or their product. For example, a politician might say they are "investing in the future" of education rather than that they are "spending money on a new building."

It is important to analyse what people say to avoid being conned or cheated.

For example: You will see or read advertisements that claim that if a person is in financial debt they will make life easier for them by consolidating their debts into one easy payment. This is generally not true as some of the debts may have lower interest payable on them or less time to run.

Keys to Critical Thinking

1. Research in depth with credible sources.

2. Identify what is being said, the topic, main points etc.

3. Comprehend, that is understand, what is being said, the terms that may have been used and the main points in the article, advertisement etc.

4. In general, question everything you read or see, including yourself. For example, what is the motive behind what is said, is the person qualified to make the statement or is it just their opinion, is it verified by facts?
    Consider a variety of options, opinions and facts.

5. Make an intelligent decision.

Communication: Multimedia

Using Multimedia

Multi-media is media and content that uses a combination of different forms in contrast to print or hand produced media. Multi-media includes a combination of any of the following:

- text
- audio
- still images
- animation
- video and interactive content form

It generally involves electronics, particularly computers.

Examples of the way multimedia might be used

A recital of a poem would be enhanced greatly by background pictures of, for example, the sun viewed at the end of a shower of rain; stars; candlelight, etc. A programme like Power Point could be used to develop the sequence of pictures necessary. A line of verse could appear with each picture. Gentle music in the background might also be added. This type of presentation impacts on more than one sense and enhances the viewer's experience.

Other forms of media might be used, for example a video camera. This might be presented as simply as *a* scene taken from one of the lines with a speaker narrating the poem.

Different Forms of Media for Different Circumstances

It is important to make sure that any presentation is suitable for the audience it is being presented to. A younger audience might prefer more visual effects but an older audience would find the same effects annoying. The nationality of the group, the information being presented to it and their educational ability is also important to consider.

In cases where the information needs to be conveyed to people of varying ages, nationalities and education, a form of comic may be a more suitable format. Even if a person can not read the instructions, the information can be presented in such a way that the pictures alone can be followed and understood.

Before you begin your presentation, you will need to consider:

- the information that needs to be conveyed. (Jot down brief points.)
- the number of frames the cartoon will contain.
- the type of person you are targeting, e.g., multi-racial, office workers, parents, etc.
- the age of the person for whom the information is intended.

Drawing comics

You can not just dash off a picture. It may take several attempts to get each frame correct. Initially draw in pencil. Do not ink until you are wholly satisfied with the whole comic.

If you are very proficient in the use of drawing tools on a computer you may use this tool, otherwise use paper. Pictures can later be scanned onto the computer.

Once you have completed each frame and are happy with it, print the words below each frame. You may type them if you have scanned in your pictures. Finally, format. Get opinions on your work from your friends or others outside your immediate family.

Contents: Using a Table of Contents

The Table of Contents is found in the front of a book or magazine and lists the chapters or articles found in the magazine or book and the pages where they can be found. It is listed in the order that the articles appear in the book.

An example of a Table of Contents is shown below. It is the contents of a Social Studies book.
The contents of a book will help you quickly decide whether or not you have found a book with the information you need.

TABLE OF CONTENTS

Diary: Writing

- A diary is a book where the events of the day are written.

- It can contain simply a list of activities.

- It may contain personal thoughts and feelings in the case of a personal diary.

- It is generally dated.

For example:

> _Monday 5th June 2014_
>
> _We visited the library and I borrowed Robinson Crusoe._
>
> _I have wanted to read this book for a long time, but haven't been able to find it until now._

Dictionary Skills

Dictionaries have come to be of help with more than just the meaning of a word and how to spell it. Many modern dictionaries now contain the following:

- Curriculum definitions,

  for example, **abstract** noun (n)
  English
  a noun having an abstract (as opposed to concrete) meaning, e.g., fear, love

e.g.,

- Variations in spelling: for example, fax is also **facsimile.**

- Etymology or the derivation of the word.

N.B. In the case of curriculum definitions you should begin by looking up the first word, e.g., abstract. If this does not work, look up the second word.

Dictionary: Uses of

You have already learnt to use a dictionary to find the meaning of words, but there are other uses of a dictionary. These include:

- to find the pronunciation or way to say difficult or new words.
- to find the part of speech, e.g., noun, verb, etc.
- to find how to spell a word and see what to add on to make the word plural.
- to find the origin of a word.
- some dictionaries help us find synonyms and antonyms.
- some dictionaries have the names of famous people.
- to find if the word needs a hyphen.

Not everything listed above may be included in a primary dictionary.

Direct or Indirect Speech: Changing To

When we quote the actual words of a speaker we use direct speech.
For example, "I am very pleased to meet you," said Jane.

When we report what has been said we use indirect speech.
For example, Jane said that she was very pleased to see me.

Rules to remember:

- Present tense becomes past tense (indirect.)

  - "How **are** (present) you?" said Mary   becomes
    Mary **asked** (past) how she was.

- Subject pronoun: First person becomes third person.

  - "**I** hope you do well in your exam, Peter," said John.   becomes
    John said **he** hoped that Peter would do well in his exam.

- Second person becomes first person or third person according to who is speaking.

  - "I hope you will come to the show," said John.   becomes
    John said **he** hoped that he would come to the show with him.

- Time: today becomes that day; yesterday becomes the previous day; tomorrow becomes the next day. (indirect)

  - "Would you like to work **today**?" said David becomes
    David asked if he would like to work **that day**.

Emails

Emails are being used increasingly over letters as they are fast and inexpensive. There are however rules that should be followed when writing them. These rules become increasingly important as you grow up and enter the workforce. They are:

- always write in sentences using correct punctuation and capitalisation. Emails without capitals and with no punctuation are hard to read. You risk the recipient deleting them.

- use proper grammar.

- never use text language.

- always re-read and correct an email before sending it.

- always finish your email with your full name, not just your Christian name. If your email is an interstate query mention your state and possibly include contact details.

- make sure if you are answering an email your answer is clear, e.g., if you are asked "Do you sell workbooks?" your answer would be "Yes, we sell workbooks."

- if asking a question make sure your question is clear and precise.

- do not attach unnecessary files.

- be careful with the formatting, structure and layout as reading from a screen is harder than reading from paper.

- answer any email swiftly. If there is a long delay explain why and apologise.

- do not forward spam, chain letters, defamatory or racial emails.

- don't reply to spam.

- if you are replying to an email leave the message thread, (previous email), rather than starting a new email. People who receive a lot of emails do not always remember the message.

- never open an email you are not sure of or one your virus checker indicates has a virus.

- never follow links unless you know who sent the email. If in doubt ask an adult.

- never answer any email promising you money that purports to come from a bank or any similar email. Simply delete.

- remember what you write may be forwarded to someone else, so never write something you would be ashamed of later or that you wouldn't want your parents to read.

Emails

- Emails are **a form of letter** which travel very quickly from one computer to another.

- They need to be written as **carefully** as letters.

- Emails have an address, a heading, a greeting, a body and a close.

- Most computers put the date and your address on for you.

Look at the email below.

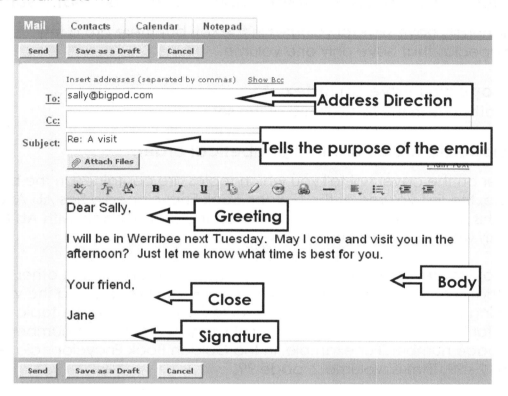

Notice the following:

- The address of the person to whom you are writing goes in the section marked "**To**...."

- Always include a reason for the letter in the "**Subject**..." People receive so many junk emails that they will often delete the email if there is no subject.

- The "Greeting" can begin with "Dear", "Hi" or "Good Morning", but there needs to be a greeting.

- The "Body" is often much shorter than a letter.

- You must have a "Close" although it need not be "Your friend." It might be "Kind Regards" or any other similar greeting.

- You are judged by the email you send. You must use capital letters and full stops. Do not use abbreviations. Although emails are often short, they are still letters and are written as such.

Using an Encyclopedia

Encyclopedias are reference books.

A reference book is a book which people refer to or look in for certain topics about which they want to know more. You will find reference books in a separate section of the library as these books are generally not allowed to be borrowed. The call number for encyclopedias is 031 and 032. The best encyclopedia for school children is probably the World Encyclopedia.

Encyclopedias are books which contain or discuss many subjects.

They generally have several volumes in the set, but there are a few encyclopedias that have only one volume.

Encyclopedias have an index.
This will often be in the last volume of the set.

Encyclopedia topics are in alphabetical order.

The letter on the cover will tell you which topics are contained in the book. For example, the first volume of the Golden Book Encyclopedia has Ab-Ar on the cover. This means it contains information on topics that begin with Ab (aborigines) and finish with Ar (archaeology).

Not all topics are easily found by this means. Many topics have other similar topics that should also be looked up. To do this you need to find the volume containing the index. It will be clearly marked on the cover. The topic you are looking for will be in alphabetical order. It will give the volume number followed by the page number. For example, in the Golden Book Encyclopedia, Australia is listed as 2 - 99, that is, volume 2, page 99.

In the Golden Book Encyclopedia, below Australia in the index are the following listings:

> climate 5 - 266
>
> farming 7 - 435
>
> flags 8 - 456
>
> forests 8 - 466
>
> gold rushes 8 - 503
>
> government 8 - 507
>
> rivers 16 - 995
>
> sheep 17 - 1047
>
> wheat 20 - 1238

All these listings relate to different aspects of Australia. You would not find these by just looking up an encyclopedia from the listings on the cover.

Hints when using an encyclopedia

1. Always look for the surname (last name) of a person. For example, Henry Lawson will be found under Lawson, Henry. You use the last name of a person when you are searching in a catalogue, dictionary, telephone book or encyclopedia.

2. If the person has a title, look for the last name of the person, not the title. For example, Captain Arthur Phillip will be found under Phillip, Captain Arthur.

3. In words of two or more parts, look for the first part. For example, for South America look for South and then America.

4. Never look for words by their abbreviations or shortened forms. For example, do not look for Mt Everest. Instead look under Mount Everest.

5. Some names begin with little prefixes such as da, Da, von, Von, de, De, la, La, van, Van. For example, da Roza, von Hindenburg, De Soto, Von Holst. If the da, la, van or von begins with a small letter, as in da Roza or von Hindenburg, look for the name under the last part, that is Roza or Hindenburg.

Envelope: Addressing

Note how an envelope is addressed below. No commas are used. The postcode is on a separate line for the Post Office sorting machine.

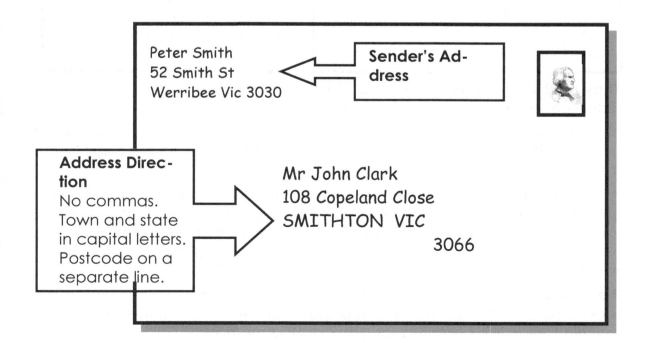

Peter Smith
52 Smith St
Werribee Vic 3030

Sender's Address

Address Direction
No commas. Town and state in capital letters. Postcode on a separate line.

Mr John Clark
108 Copeland Close
SMITHTON VIC
                3066

Index

An index is found in the back of a book. It is arranged in alphabetical order. The contents of a book outlines the chapters in a book but an index is far more detailed. It is very useful as it tells you on what page you can find a more detailed list of topics.

For example: A simple index might be similar to that shown below, but it would be much longer.

adverbs 38, 39	invitations 8 - 11
conjunctions 18	nouns 4
continents 42	invitations 8 - 11
homonyms 30 - 31	reading for information 42, 43

To use a simple index like the example above, look through in alphabetical order for the topic you want.

A simple index lists topics only by page numbers, but some indexes are more complex. For example:

Abacus 1 - 3, 5 - 291	African Animals 1 - 21
Abbreviations 1 - 3	elephants 7 - 395
Aborigines 1 - 4, 1 - 59, 2 - 100, 3 - 133	giraffe 8 - 497
Bennelong 3 - 143	hippopotamus 9 - 547
boomerangs 3 - 143	hyena 10 - 580
cooking 5 - 306	lion 11 - 689
myths and legends 13 - 806	rhinoceros 16 - 991
Namatjira 13 - 810	zebra 20 - 162
Phillip 15 - 919	Agriculture see Farming
Acacia 20 - 1223	Air 1 - 25

- **They may list topics under several different headings**, e.g., ants may be listed under ants, insects or under both.

- If the index is for an encyclopedia or a similar book where there are several volumes, then the index will list the volume number first and the page number second.

- In a complex index, such as the one above, the main topics are listed in alphabetical order, but below the topic further suggestions related to the topic are often included. For example: Below aborigines are pages that might be referred to for more specific topics, like boomerangs and cooking methods.

- **The index may also refer you to other parts of the index.**
  For example: Below aborigines are pages that might be referred to for more specific topics, like boomerangs and cooking methods.

- **The index may list the topic under a different name.**
  For example: "Agriculture see Farming" means that articles on this topic are listed under Farming.

Invitation: Writing

Before you write an invitation you must ask yourself the following questions:

Who is being invited? A family or just a friend.

What? What are you inviting people to: a barbecue, a dinner, a party?

Where? Where is it being held?

When? When is it being held?

Why? What is the reason: a birthday, a get-together?

How? People want to know how to dress. If it is a barbecue, the dress will be casual but if it is a party the dress will be more formal.

Often at the bottom the letters **R.S.V.P.** will appear. This is French for please reply if you please.

Below is a very simple invitation. Often it will be sent on a card. Read the invitation carefully.

When you receive an invitation, it is very rude not to answer it even if you cannot attend. Parties need to be prepared for and the host or hostess need to know exactly how many people are coming.

John Smith's 60th Birthday Party

To: The Jones Family | Who? |

Please come and help us celebrate the 60th Birthday of John Smith. | What? | | Why? |

Where: 56 Yandaloo Place, Smithton Vic 3757 | Where? |

When: 21st July 2014, 5pm - 11pm | When? |

A buffet meal will be provided. Please bring soft drinks. | How? |

R.S.V.P. by 30th June 2014 to Mary Smith, 40 Glenelg Crt, Westhampton, Vic 3756 or phone 57289656.

Invitation: Answering

While many invitations, such as the ones on the previous page include a phone number, it is polite to send a written reply when you receive a written invitation.

Remember, every letter must have a heading, a date, a greeting, a body, a close and a signature.

The Heading
This contains your address as you are the person writing the letter.

52 Smith St,
Westhampton, Vic, 3757 **Date**

20th June, 2014

Greeting

Dear Mary,

Thank you for your kind invitation. Jane, Peter, John, Rosemary and
I will be pleased to come and celebrate Uncle John's **Body** 60th birthday on
21st July with you.

If we can help in any way with the preparation and set up, please let us know.

Kind regards to all,
Veronica Jones. **Close**

Signature

There are some things that are important to remember when answering an invitation:

1. Reply to the name and address written beside the R.S.V.P.

2. Mention the date of the party.

3. Reply on behalf of the person or persons invited. In this case all of the Jones family were invited, so the reply must be on behalf of the whole family. Instead of "Jane, Peter, John, Rosemary and I" you could have written, "The Jones family."

4. A different close could be used, e.g., "Yours sincerely", "Your friend" or "With regards".

Letter: Writing a Business Letter

A business letter has a different format to a letter written to a friend. The letter is written more formally and a business letter includes both your address and the business you are writing to.

Read carefully through the letter below.

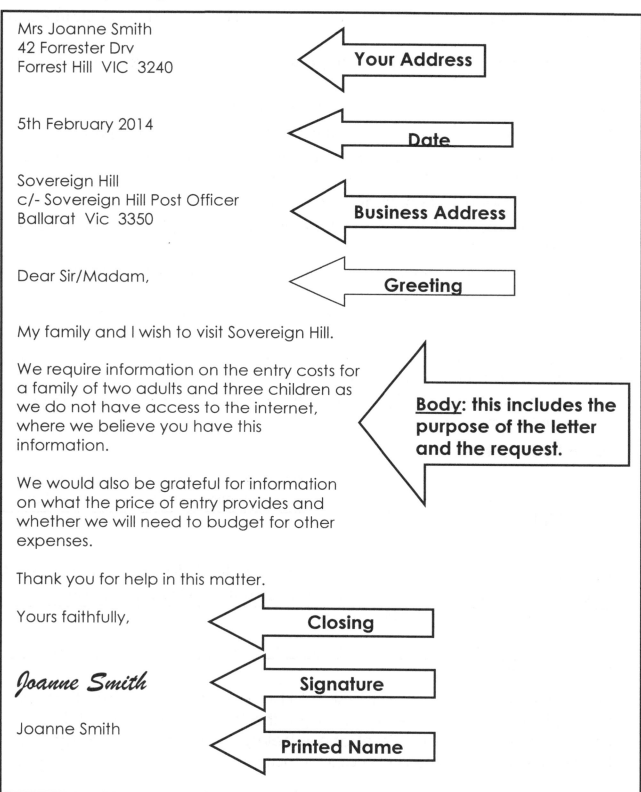

Mrs Joanne Smith
42 Forrester Drv
Forrest Hill VIC 3240

Your Address

5th February 2014

Date

Sovereign Hill
c/- Sovereign Hill Post Officer
Ballarat Vic 3350

Business Address

Dear Sir/Madam,

Greeting

My family and I wish to visit Sovereign Hill.

We require information on the entry costs for a family of two adults and three children as we do not have access to the internet, where we believe you have this information.

Body: this includes the purpose of the letter and the request.

We would also be grateful for information on what the price of entry provides and whether we will need to budget for other expenses.

Thank you for help in this matter.

Yours faithfully,

Closing

Joanne Smith

Signature

Joanne Smith

Printed Name

Letter: Writing to the Editor

Newspapers contain letters written by the general public to the newspaper commenting on various issues, which can vary widely. The most common topics include:

- supporting or opposing an editorial stance
- responding to another writer's letter to the editor
- commenting on current issues being debated by the Federal or State Parliaments
- remarking on a news story that appeared in a previous issue, either critically or positively
- correcting a perceived error or misrepresentation

Letters to the Editor are usually required to be <u>no more than 200 words.</u>

An effective persuasive letter will only result after consideration of the following points, although not all may apply in every situation:

- What is the idea, issue or change you are promoting?
- Who is the intended audience? What are the beliefs, problems and preferences of your audience?
- What possible objections may prevent your reader from responding favourably?
- What questions are likely to be asked about your proposed change or idea?
- What benefits can the reader gain from accepting your idea? How can you best demonstrate these benefits?
- What specific action do you want the reader to take and when do you want them to take it?

Draft Your Letter

- In your first sentence you need to establish a bond with the reader, a central appeal which serves as a foundation on which to build your case. For example:

> ### Education
>
> Education is a vital tool for equipping students for the workplace. A National Curriculum can deliver this, but it must be carefully
planned and not rushed through.

2. Present you argument to convince your reader of what you are proposing. For example:

> The curriculum for each grade should be released a year at a time, ensuring that students have been taught the foundational material they need rather than dramatic changes being made to eleven grades at once. It is easy to write a curriculum that suggests that students should

3. Close by stating clearly the action you would like your readers to take. For example:

> I urge families concerned about the future education of their children to contact their local Members of Parliament and request that they take the necessary time to review the National Curriculum before implementing it.

Letter: Writing a Friendly Letter

Every letter must have <u>a heading, a date, a greeting, a body, a close and a signature.</u>

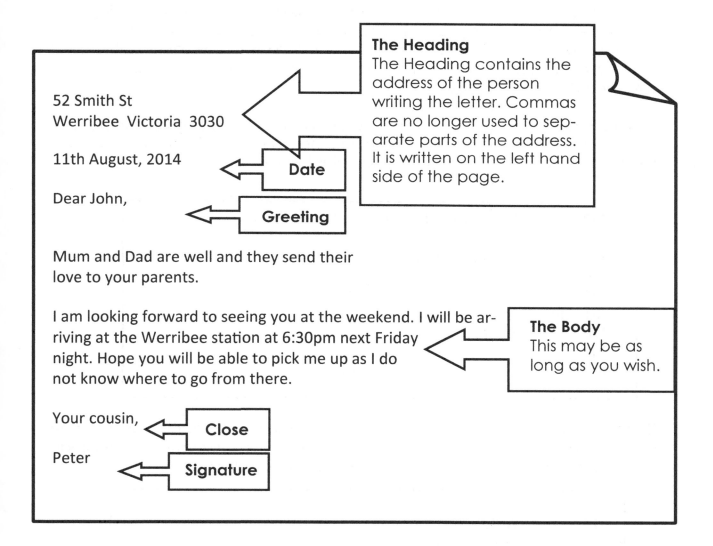

52 Smith St
Werribee Victoria 3030

11th August, 2014

Dear John,

Mum and Dad are well and they send their love to your parents.

I am looking forward to seeing you at the weekend. I will be arriving at the Werribee station at 6:30pm next Friday night. Hope you will be able to pick me up as I do not know where to go from there.

Your cousin,

Peter

Date

Greeting

Close

Signature

The Heading
The Heading contains the address of the person writing the letter. Commas are no longer used to separate parts of the address. It is written on the left hand side of the page.

The Body
This may be as long as you wish.

Library: How Books Are Arranged

While information can be found on the internet, it is not always easy to know if the information is accurate or if it is simply someone's opinion. Books such as those found in libraries, are published and the publisher generally checks to make sure that the information in the book is accurate. In a library you can often find several books on a topic and compare the facts in them to see if they agree.

Classification of Books

Books in libraries are arranged in two main categories: **fiction** (stories) and **non-fiction** (facts). These two categories are separated. Fiction is labeled using the first three letters of the author's surname, for example, Enid Blyton would be indexed as BLY.

Non-fiction is arranged differently. It is arranged according to topics using the Dewey Decimal Classification. It is called Dewey because the system was invented by Melville Dewey. It is called a decimal system because a little dot or decimal point (.) is used. It is called classification because the books are arranged in classes or topics.

You have an address where you live, so people can easily find you. Books also have an address that helps you find them. The first part of the address tells you the category or topic. Look at the examples below:

030	Encyclopedias and Dictionaries
359	Navies
491	Modern Languages
520	Astronomy (sun, moon, etc.)
580	Botany (trees, plants, flowers, seeds, etc.)
781, 785	Dance Music
770	Photography
900	History
910	Geography and Travel

There are a lot of books under each category. The books are then given further numbers, similar to your house number, and these will come after the decimal. These numbers are "call numbers." Look at the examples below:

595	Ants
591.9	Desert Animals
808.81	Children's Poetry
994	Australian History

These numbers make it easy to find a book.

Library: Finding a Book

1. Knowing how books in a library are classified is only the first step in finding a book.

2. Most libraries have computers where all the information you need to find a book is stored.

3. A librarian will always help you find the information you want, but librarians are busy people, so it is good to know how to look the information up yourself.

4. When you look at the computer in the library to search for books, it will have the words, **"Basic Search"** on the screen. The information will look like this:

   Title: the title is the name of the book.

   Author: the author is the person who wrote the book.

5. If you are looking for fiction, then you may know either the title or the author. if you know either of these you can type them into one of the first two boxes. You would generally type in the author's name if you were looking for other books written by him/her. Always type the author's last name first.

Title Keyword: ....

Author (last name, first name): ....

General Keyword: ....

Subject Browse: ....

General Keywords
You will use this section if you are looking for non-fiction. You need to type words into the box that describe what you are looking for, e.g., Ancient History Romans. (Do not put in commas or small words like "and" or "the". It confuses the computer.)

Once you have entered the "General Keywords" hit "enter" and the computer will come up with a list of books in the category. This may be a very long list, so it is best to write down the first three numbers, which will give you the category, and then the next three numbers that follow the decimal point. Of course, if you see a book listed that is exactly what you are looking for, write down the whole address.

Subject
The subject is the main topic, for example, dogs.

Searching
1. Once you have found the general area you need to search, go to the shelves.

2. If you have call numbers you will need the non-fiction section. The numbers will begin at 0 on the left hand side of the first shelf and run down towards the right.

3. Numbers always run from left to right. If you are looking for 915, you should go to the last row of shelves.

4. Look for the first three numbers first. Once you have found the first three numbers you can then begin looking for the numbers after the decimal point.

5. There may be several books with this number or there may be only one. You can then check each book until you find the information you are looking for.

What happens if you can not find a book?

- Sometimes the book you want is stored at another library or is already lent to another borrower.
- Speak to the librarian and she/he will help you reserve the book.

Borrowing a book

- Anyone can look at books in a library, but to borrow books you will need a library card. If you do not have one, your parents will need to fill out the forms to apply for one.

- The library card has a number which tells the librarian who has the book and when it will be returned.

- Once you have found the book you want you will need to take it to the librarian, along with your library card, and she/he will record the number and tell you the date when the book must be returned.

- Alternatively some libraries now have machines where you can scan in your card and the book yourself.

- If the book you wish to borrow is not in your library you may put in a request for an inter-library loan. This can be aided if you can find, via means of the internet, another library that has the book. N.B. It will usually take several weeks to obtain the book.

Media—Multimedia

Multi-media is media and content that uses a combination of different forms in contrast to print or hand produced media. Multi-media includes a combination of any of the following: text, audio, still images, animation, video and interactive content form. It generally involves electronics, particularly computers.

A recital of a poem would be enhanced greatly by background pictures of, for example, the sun viewed at the end of a shower of rain; stars; candlelight, etc. A programme like Power Point could be used to develop the sequence of pictures necessary. A line of verse could appear with each picture. Gentle music in the

Magazines

Magazines are publications, generally published on a regular basis, containing a variety of articles. Each magazine aims at a particular market, e.g., women, finances, craft etc. Magazines are generally paid for by advertising.

Media: Cartoons

It is important to make sure that any presentation is suitable for the audience it is being presented to. A younger audience might prefer more visual effects but an older audience would find the same effects annoying. The nationality of the group the information is being presented to and their educational ability is also important to consider.

In cases where the information needs to be conveyed to people of varying ages, nationalities and education, a form of comic may be a more suitable format. Even if a person can not read the instructions, the information can be presented in such a way that the pictures alone can be followed.

Before you begin your presentation, you will need to consider:

- the information that needs to be conveyed. (Jot down brief points.)
- the number of frames the cartoon will contain.
- the type of person you are targeting, e.g., multi-racial, office workers, parents, etc.
- the age of the person for whom the information is intended.

You can not just dash off a picture. It may take several attempts to get each frame correct. Initially draw in pencil. Do not ink until you are wholly satisfied with the whole comic.

If you are very proficient in the use of drawing tools on a computer you may use this tool, otherwise use paper. Pictures can later be scanned onto the computer.

Once you have completed each frame and are happy with it, print the words below each frame. You may type them if you have scanned in your pictures. Finally format. Get opinions on your work from your friends or others outside your immediate family.

Multimedia: Social Networking

Social Networking

Social networking is expanding the number of one's friends or business contacts. With the introduction of the internet many online services or sites that reflect social relations among people with common interests have sprung up, e.g., Facebook, MySpace and Twitter.

Facebook

Facebook is an internet sites where a person can keep up to date details about themselves and their activities which their friends can access easily. A person can upload photos, publish notes, get the latest news from their friends or even post videos. No private information should ever be placed on a site or personal comments about other people.

There are basic rules for using Facebook and other social networking sites. These are:

- be careful who you "friend."
- restrict the number of friends who have access to your site
- a public profile, available to others, should contain virtually no other details other than your name and the information that the profile is only available to friends.
- never write anything or put up photos that you would be unhappy for your parents, grandparents or strangers to view.
- make sure your computer is protected by antivirus software.

Disadvantages and Problems

- anything placed on the internet while it can be deleted can never be totally removed.
- people tend to update these sites rather than contacting friends personally, so rather than drawing people together it can isolate them. People are becoming more dependent on these technological ways of communicating. Personal, one to one conversations are really important in our everyday life.
- with these sites people's knowledge of each other tends to be more superficial.
- "friends" can copy your pictures and information and put them on other sites. You then have no control over the contents and can not remove them.
- people can become addicted to these sites and spend too much time on them, diminishing their daily lives and social skills and isolating them.
- a lot of drama can occur on these sites and things said can be easily misinterpreted.
- there is a huge threat of viruses. Some of the viruses allow information to be stolen from the site. Identity theft is becoming too common.
- emails are often sent from anonymous users asking to "friend" or seeking personal information.

- scammers can trick people to get their details. This is done through 'phishing' websites that look similar to Facebook.
- what is written on these sites is increasingly being used as evidence in courts. The idea that you are free to say on these sites what you wouldn't say in person is erroneous.
- employers are increasingly scanning the internet to find information on prospective employees. What is written at 15 years old may haunt you at 30.
- these sites are leading to a narcisstic generation who believe the world is interested in the smallest thing they do or feel, e.g., having a cup of coffee.

Twitter

Twitter is an online social networking and microblogging service that enables its users to send and read text based posts of up to 140 characters. These are informally known as "tweets."

Twitter is easy to use and can be joined very quickly. "Message boards" or tweets can be viewed in public. It can be a great business platform and helps businesses understand their market and identify competitors' strategies by following their tweets.

Its greatest disadvantage is it is the main site for spammers.

Blogging

A blog is a type of website or part of a website. Blogs are usually maintained by an individual with entries containing commentaries, description of events or other material such as graphics. Entries are usually displayed in reverse-chronological order. Most blogs are usually interactive, allowing visitors to leave comments and messages.

Many blogs provide commentary on news or a particular subject. A typical blog contains text, images and links to other blogs. Some of the advantages are that a blog can be developed simply. A blog post is available to anyone who can search the internet. It is very convenient so people tend to use it more frequently. It can help improve writing as blog sites have to be of a reasonable standard and individuals can learn to express their opinions and exchange views on topics.

Among its disadvantages are the necessity to own a computer and the time it takes to regularly update an entry. Regular writing may give rise to slang and bad writing which takes away from the quality of the blog. Not all information can be shared on blog sites and therefore information may be biased or incomplete. There is no confidentiality as it is a public forum and it is important to make sure that blogs or comments are based on fact that can be substantiated and are not slanderous or the writer may be sued. It is not suited for issues requiring immediate solutions as there is a time lapse before comments appear.

This type of presentation impacts on more than one sense and enhances the viewer's experience.

Other forms of media might be used, for example a video camera. This might be presented as simply as a scene taken from one of the lines with a speaker

Newspapers

It is possible to read thousands of different newspapers on the net from a variety of countries. There is a risk that they will eventually be devoured by the net. This could then lead to a control of information that is fed to the public. This already happens in countries like China.

Films, Music and Broadband

All these media are available on the internet. There is a growing list available for downloading, including books that have been out of print for many years. It is important to make sure before you download anything that you are not using a pirated copy or breaking copyright. This is stealing. If enough people steal from film makers and music producers they will go out of business and no more will be produced.

Newspaper: Main Elements

There are five common characteristics you will find in almost all articles that you read in newspapers or on the internet. They are:

1. **Headline**
   The title of the article. It is designed to catch the reader's attention and is usually not a complete sentence. Instead it will try to summarise the main idea of the article. It is usually printed in bold and often in larger letters. The main words will have capitals.

   For example: **Tiger eats Man**

2. **Byline**
   This line tells you who has written the article and may also include the address of the author and the publication or news source for which he or she writes. e.g., John Smith, Age Investigative Unit.

3. **Location**
   This is usually placed at the beginning of the article. If the city or location is well known, e.g., Canberra, the name alone will be written. If the city is less famous more information may be included. Sometimes only the position of a person who works at the paper, e.g., Health Reporter, is included.

4. **Lead Paragraph**
   It is usually placed at the beginning of an article in bold print. The lead briefly answers the questions "who", "what", "where", and "how". This is the skeleton of the story.

5. **Supporting Paragraphs**
   These are the paragraphs that follow the lead. They develop the ideas introduced by the lead and give more explanations, details or quotes. They may continue on later pages.

Newspaper: Reporting an Event

A newspaper writes articles each day to inform us of events taking place within Australia and the world. Community newspaper are printed once a week and inform us of events that happen in the community.

When you write to inform, you should aim to provide information in a way that:

- tells the reader what he or she needs, wants or would like to know.

- supplies answers to questions such as who, what, why, where, when and how.

- gives information that is balanced and explains the facts rather than trying to persuade the reader of a particular view. To do this the writer will need to make the facts easy to understand.

- is clear and interesting.

- is not too large but which covers all the important events.

To report an event work through the following steps:

1. Make sure you have all the details regarding the event that took place, e.g., where, when, what happened etc.

2. Decide which details of the event you will use, e.g., in reporting an ANZAC Day parade you might report on only one contingent, e.g., Malaya-Borneo Veterans.

3. Jot down all the details you wish to include.

4. Write a number beside each idea in the order you want to use them.

5. Make up sentences using your ideas and following the number sequence you have given them.

6. Check your work. Make any corrections necessary.

7. Decide which sentences belong together in a paragraph. Although the newspaper article will be shorter than other forms of writing, it should still have a beginning, middle and end.

8. Read through your work and check it. Also check:
   a. there are at least two sentences in each paragraph.
   b. you began a new paragraph for each new idea.
   c. there is a conclusion to your article.

9. Choose a title for your article. It needs to be catchy, e.g., "Jack and Jill Have an Accident."

Note Taking

When you research a topic you will not remember everything you read so it is important to be able to take notes.

Here are some points to help you.

1. Look over the section you are interested in quickly, keeping in mind your topic. It is always important to read passages before making notes.

2. Title the notes. For example, "Football". Date the notes.

3. Write the author's name, title of the book, publishing company, place of publication and the date published (Bibliography). It is important to note that some old books do not contain the date of publication.

4. Write an outline containing the main thoughts in the passage.

5. Fill in the outline with key words and phrases. Never use a phrase where you can use a word.

6. Do not write everything you read.

7. Never keep notes on scraps of paper. Have paper that can be filed in a folder or use an exercise book.

In the passage below the underlined words show what would have been written as notes.

As <u>land</u> was <u>explored</u> in early New South Wales it was made <u>available</u> for <u>sheep</u> and <u>cattle</u>. <u>Wide expanses</u> of land were <u>taken up</u> by these men and prior to the gold rush they <u>provided</u> welcome <u>income</u> from the sale of <u>wool</u>. These men were later termed <u>squatters</u>, since they had established runs to which they had <u>no land title</u>. The old dream of the <u>Colony</u> becoming dotted with small farms and becoming <u>self-sufficient</u> did <u>not happen</u>.

The <u>squatters</u> did not need to <u>buy land</u>. As time progressed they <u>paid a minimal rent</u> to the Government. They <u>did not improve</u> the <u>land</u>, cultivate it or settle down. Instead they <u>put</u> their <u>money into stock</u>. When the <u>land</u> was <u>worn out</u> they simply <u>moved on</u>.

This did not please the Government. <u>Settlement</u> was <u>spreading</u> <u>further</u> and further out and the <u>Government could not control or protect</u> the squatters. There was also an <u>alarming growth</u> in the amount of <u>land</u> being <u>taken up by</u> men in the <u>upper class in society</u>. So the <u>Government</u> began passing laws to <u>restrict</u> further <u>growth</u>.

Newspaper: Reading

Newspapers have been a source of information for hundreds of years. Some of the early newspapers were called broadsheets and generally contained scurrilous information about well know figures in the community.

Different types of newspapers serve different purposes. Some appear daily and , some appear weekly. They contain more news than either the nightly news on television or the news on the radio, both of which are limited by time.

There are three main types of newspapers:

- a national newspaper, e.g., the Australian, containing national news
- daily newspapers, e.g., Courier Mail, Morning Herald, Herald Sun, Advertiser, the Western Australian, all of which focus more on state news. These will often contain more "gossipy" type news and personal articles than the national newspaper.
- community newspapers that appear weekly and keep the local community in touch with what is happening in the area.

Most daily newspapers will contain the following:

- lead (important) articles on the first page
- national news—this is limited in all but the Australian
- state news
- world news
- specialist articles that may appear occasionally, weekly or only once
- advertising—this largely pays for the paper's running costs
- weather
- television guides
- sport news and events
- job advertisements
- personal columns

Community newspapers will only contain:

- state news, if it applies to the local community, e.g., funds have been approved for a new school
- community news
- personal articles about people in the community
- advertising—this largely pays for the paper's running costs
- sports news and events
- real estate information
- car sales
- job vacancies
- personal columns and advertisements

Notes: Expanding

To expand notes you add words to make the notes into sentences. Look carefully at the example below.

Squatter purchase run where improvements, e.g., house, shed, dam, cleared area.
Squatters improvements land wanted keep

Selector hard time.
Afford only half land.
Some not suitable cultivation
Land needed house, shed, pens.

A **squatter** had the right to **purchase** the part of his **run** on which he had made **improvements**: built a **house**, a shearing **shed**, sunk a **dam** or **cleared timber**. Squatters would often quickly make improvements on the sections of land they wanted to keep before the selector came.

The genuine free selector had a hard time. Often he could not afford to select 320 acres and had to settle for half the amount. Some of this land might not be suitable for cultivation. Then some of the land needed to be used for a house, shed and pens for the animals.

Reading a Menu

- Every café or restaurant has a menu.

- The menu tells you what food and drinks are available.

- It is important to read the menu carefully before making a choice.

Sometimes you may be charged more for what you want, e.g., a toasted ham and cheese sandwich may cost 50 cents more if you add in tomato, onion or pineapple.

Sometimes, for example with main meals, salad or salad and chips may be included in the price. The menu is usually for those who sit down and eat at the restaurant. Takeaway food is cheaper. It is usually displayed on a

Reading a Timetable

- A Timetable gives you information about a schedule.

- It might tell you when a bus or a train runs, when a football or basketball team are to play and where or what hours someone is to work and on what days.

The table below is part of the timetable from Manor Lake to Werribee Shopping Centre. Often the two timetables will be printed on opposite sides of a sheet of paper. Each timetable shows the schedule for the morning and the schedule for the afternoon separately.

Time of bus p.m.

Feathertop Drive	9.00	9.38	10.16	10.54	11.32	12.20
Smith St	9.10	9.48	10.26	11.04	11.42	12.30
Ballan Rd	9.20	9.58	10.36	11.14	11.52	12.40
Shorts Rd	9.30	10.08	10.46	11.24	12.02	12.50
Railway Av	9.40	10.18	10.56	11.34	12.12	1.00
Watton St	9.50	10.28	11.06	11.44	12.22	1.10

To read the timetable:

- Find the correct timetable.

- Look down the list for the stop you wish to get on, e.g., Smith St

- Look across the timetable for the possible times to catch the bus, e.g., 9.48 p.m.

- If you wish to tell a friend when you will arrive, find the stop you are getting on, then the time you are catching the bus. Run your finger down the column until you come to the stop you wish to get off.
  For example, get on Feathertop Drive 10.54 p.m. Alight Railway Ave 11.34 p.m.

Reading and Using a Timeline

A timeline can be another useful way to enhance a report. Look at the following examples of early discoverers:

```
1642        Abel Tasman discovered Tasmania

1788        First Fleet arrived at Botany Bay

1616        Dirk Hartog landed in Western Australia

1688        William Dampier landed in Western Australia

1804        Hobart Town established in Van Diemen's Land
```

The list above are simply facts. They can be better represented by the timeline below. The oldest date is written at the bottom.

```
1804 —— Hobart Town established in Van Diemen's Land

1788 —— First Fleet landed at Sydney Cove

1688 —— William Dampier landed in Western Australia

1642 —— Abel Tasman discovered Tasmania

1616 —— Dirk Hartog landed in Western Australia
```

Map Reading

A map must show:

- **a title** (This tells you what you are looking at.)
- **scale** (This tells you the distance.)
- **compass points** (This shows direction.)
- **key** (This shows you what the pictures you are looking at represent.)
- **grid** (This enables you to find specific places.)

The **grid** helps you to find specific places. When you look up a street in an index it will give you a grid reference. This reference will contain a letter followed by a number, e.g., B5.

- Run your right hand across the top of the map until you find B.
- Run your left hand down the side of the page until you find 5.
- Run your left hand finger across and your right hand finger down until they meet. This is the street you are seeking - Branch Street.
- Sometimes the reference is not exactly at this point but it will be very close.

The **key** shows you what the pictures on the map represent.

Scale tells you the distance.

The **compass** shows direction.

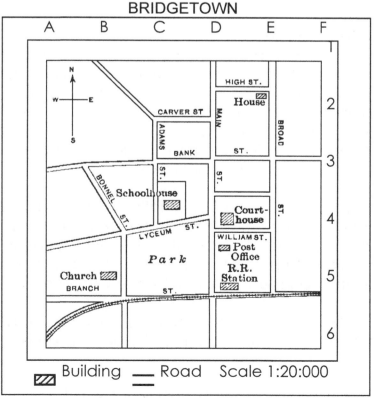

Referencing

When you quote from a passage you are required to acknowledge the source of the information. There are now several methods of doing this, but only one of these is shown below. You will learn about others in later years.

You need to identify references for three reasons:
- a. to prove what you have written has a factual basis.
- b. to show the research that has been done to reach your conclusions, for example, in a report.
- c. to allow the reader to identify and retrieve the references for their own use.

The Notation System

This system has been used for at least a hundred years and is, in my opinion, the clearest system. Should you go to TAFE or University it is best to check with your tutor to see which system he/she prefers.

To quote directly from a book or document, enclose the quote in quotation marks and put a superscript number after it. In the footnote at the bottom of the page write the number and include the author, the title of the book and the page number. The full details will be shown in the back of the work in the Bibliography.

Look at the example below.

> Discoveries of gold at Ballarat and Bendigo were on a larger scale than anywhere in New South Wales and caused a big rush. Melbourne and Geelong soon lost a large part of their male population and in a few weeks at least 6,000 people were at the diggings. This population was added to by a rush from overseas and in September 1852 alone, 19,000 people landed in Melbourne and headed for the gold fields.
>
> With so many diggers arriving at the goldfields there was not enough permanent housing. "The digger's residence was commonly a small calico tent on the slopes of the gully where the claim was, and the area occupied was twelve by eight (feet).....The furniture consisted of one or two stumps for trees, while anything in the shape of a box served for a table."[1]
>
> Even as late as 1861, one third of Victoria's population lived in tents and huts. However gradually these were replaced by permanent buildings with gardens and parks.
>
> [1] The History of Bendigo, Stewart and Murray, p 5

Thesaurus

A Thesaurus is a useful book. <u>It is a dictionary of synonyms and antonyms</u>. You will find it very useful when you are writing.

You can use a thesaurus to find:

- an alternative word for an overused one, e.g., nice, good.
- a more formal word for an everyday word, e.g., complex instead of hard.
- a more specific word for a general one, e.g., jacket or parka instead of coat.
- the names for the male, female or young of some animals.
- the opposite of many words.

A thesaurus is:

- generally laid out in alphabetical order.
- the first word of each entry, the "headword" or "keyword" is printed in bold.
- the part of speech, e.g., verb, adjective, follows the headword, e.g., coat *noun.*
- synonyms are shown underneath the headword.
- where there are several meanings of the word, they are shown below each other and a sentence showing the meaning may be given.
- antonyms for some of the words are given below the headword and synonyms. These may be labeled as "antonym, opposite or contrasting words."
- some entries may have a cross reference printed below them and may be shown as "see" or "see also."

An entry in a thesaurus will look something like the one below:

---

coat *noun*
1. (*kinds of coats*) anorak, blazer, dinner jacket, duffle coat, mackintosh, parka, topcoat, windcheater, wrap. See also: cloak
2. *an animal's coat.* fleece, fur, hair, hide, pelt, skin.
3. *a coat of paint.* coating, cover, film, layer. **coat** *verb*
He coated the chair with paint. The car was coated with mud.

Understanding Poetry

Poets and their times

Poets reflect the events and ideas of their times through their poetry. An understanding of the time the poetry was written may lead to an understanding of the poet's ideas. Knowledge of the poet's background also gives us an insight.

1. **Analysing Poetry**

   - Every poem will have a **theme** or main idea. It will convey the **message** or **intentions** of the poet.

   - It may be a **narrative** which tells a story, or a **lyric** which describes the personal feelings of the poet.

2. **Form**

   - A poem is written in a particular form. Poems are usually written in lines and these may be grouped in stanzas (verses), although this is not necessarily so. Free verse has no restrictions.

   Sentence structure may be altered slightly in poetry and there are **enjambment** or run-on lines. These occur at the end of a line where there is no punctuation. The sense continues into the next line and the poet's thoughts remain unbroken.

3. **Diction or Word Choice**

   The poet's use of words creates the mood or atmosphere and sets the poem in its correct context, that is, its correct time and place.

   - Word choice can influence the rhythm of the poem.

   - In a rhyming poem, appropriate word choice is crucial.

   - Jargon and slang may be used for effect.

   - The use of repetition is also an effective device.

4. **Tone**

   - The tone of the poem will reveal the poet's subjective views and attitudes.

   - The tone helps to create the desired mood or atmosphere. This is achieved by word choice, rhythm and the sound of words.

   - As in literature, the tone may be friendly, scary, angry etc.

5. **Rhythm**

   Poetry often has a rhythm or flow and in this way is similar to music.

   - the rhythm sets the pace of the poem and should match the meaning.

   - a slow rhythm would enforce a sombre meaning and a quicker pace rhythm could reflect a happier mood.

   - poetic sound devices influence the pace and pause of the rhythm.

6. **Rhyme**

   Rhyme depends on the sound, not sight, and is frequently used by poets. Two consequently rhyming lines are called a **couplet**.

"There was an old woman, as I've heard tell,
She went to market her eggs for to sell;"

A four lined poem is called a **quatrain**.

Piping down the valley wild,
Piping songs of pleasant glee,
On a cloud I saw a child,
And he laughing said to me,
"Happy Songs" by William Blake

N.B. Lines 1 and 3 rhyme and lines 2 and 4.

7. **Imagery**

Imagery, often involving the senses, conjures up word pictures. It achieves this through a combination of literal and figurative language.

8. **Metre**

Metre is the number of stresses or beats in a line of poetry.

He clasps/ the crag/ with crooked/hands:
Close/to the sun/ in lonely/ lands,
Ringed/ with the azure/ world,/ he stands.
"The Eagle" by Lord Tennyson

Metre creates special effects to suit the mood of the poem. It can give a physical effect or create movement as in the last line of the "The Eagle",
"And/like a thunderbolt,/ he falls".

Writing Checklist

1. **Identify the genre or style of writing required:**

Is it a report, a story, a poem, etc.? Make sure you understand what is required for each genre.

2. **Story Writing, Report Writing, Autobiography, Biography:**

- Make sure you understand your topic.

- Ask any of the following questions that apply:

    a. **Who** is the story about?

    b. **What** is the plot or main event in the story? Always jot down any ideas you have on a spare sheet of paper. Never try to keep them in your head.

    c. **Where** is it set?

    d. **When** does it take place?

    e. **How?** The process that was undertaken.

    f. **Characters:** Who is the main character or characters? Are there other important characters? Outline them.

3. **For all types of writing:**

- **Jot** down any ideas on a sheet of paper.
- **Read** them through and **number** them in the order you wish to use them. **Cross out** any that are not appropriate.
- Create an **outline** from these notes.
- **Expand** your ideas by creating sentences using the ideas, but still following the sequence in your outline.
- You must have a **beginning**, a **middle** and a **conclusion** or **end**.

4. **Check** your work for the following:

- Are there at least two sentences in a paragraph?
- Do your sentences begin in different ways for interest and are they of different length?
- Do your sentences build on the previous ones and are they clear?
- Have you spelt correctly?
- Is all your writing in the first person, second person etc.?
- Are you writing in the past, present or future tense correctly?
- Have you used correct capitalization and punctuation?
- Does your beginning or introduction catch the reader's attention?
- If you are writing a story or a biography, have you developed your character sufficiently?

- If you are writing a story does it reach a climax before the final ending?
- Have you brought your writing to a logical conclusion or have you left it hanging?
- If there is a dialogue, do you have quotation marks around the conversation and does each new conversation begin on another line?
- If you are writing a report have you included all the relevant facts? Should you add or delete any?
- Each time you had a new idea did you start a new paragraph?
- Can you add adjectives or adverbs that will make the writing more vivid? (Don't over do it.)
- No sentences are begun with "but", "and" or "however".
- Have some words been used too frequently? Use a thesaurus to find words that could be used instead.
- Is your handwriting legible?

Writing: Autobiography

An autobiography is a history of a person's life written or told by that person.

When writing an autobiography:

- Be yourself. It is alright to be funny.
- Avoid clichés.
- Decide what key points make up your history. Include these points and make them interesting
- Read through what you have written.
- Jot down any other ideas you have on a piece of paper.
- Write your story first on a sheet of paper.
- When you are sure that it is correct, copy it onto your book and then draw a picture of yourself.

To help you start your writing, answer the questions below about yourself.

1. I am _____ years old.

2. I was born on _____. (date)

3. I am a _____ (boy or girl).

4. I have _____ brothers and _____ sisters.

5. I live in _____ (town) in _____. (state)

6. Write notes for a brief description of yourself.

    _____

    _____

    _____

    _____

7. I like to eat _____

    _____

8. List activities you enjoy. _____

    _____

    _____

9. Special things about me: _____

    _____

© Valerie Marett and Carmel Musumeci
Coroneos Publications

Australian Homeschooling #567
English Handbook

Writing: Biography

Some of the things you may learn about a person in a biography or autobiography are:

- where a person was born
- where they grew up
- what they look like
- what they like and dislike
- what they enjoy doing
- what they work as, if they are grown up
- what they are famous for—if they are well known

To help you begin writing, answer the questions below:
(You do not need to write in sentences.)

1. The name of the person.

2. Their appearance.

3. When and where they were born.

4. If they had brother or sisters.

5. Where they grew up.

6. Where they live now.

7. Where they worked and what they did.

8. Some of their early experiences.

9. What events changed or shaped their life? Did these become obstacles or did they learn from them?

10. Changes they have seen over the years.

11. Special things about them.

12. List adjectives that describe the person.

Make sure you do plenty of research on the person before you write about them. Keep a bibliography containing the book, author, year printed, and publisher. If you intend to use quotes, note the page the quote was taken from.

To write the biography:

1. Decide how much of the information you have gained about the person you will use. Put aside any information you do not need.

2. Jot down key points you wish to use on a piece of paper.

3. Write a number beside each idea in the order you want to use them.

4. Make up sentences using your ideas and follow the number sequence you have given them.

5. Decide which sentences belong together in a paragraph.

6. Remember you must have a beginning or introduction, a middle and an end.

   My example:
   Introduction: name, where he/she lives, brothers and sisters

   Middle or main part of autobiography:

       a. where born, grew up, early life, any early experiences,

       b. as they grew older where they worked and what they did

       c. changes they have seen over the years

   End or Conclusion: the type of person they are now, special things about them.

7. Read through your rough draft and check it. Also check:

   a. there are at least two sentences in each paragraph.

   b. you began a new paragraph for each new idea.

   c. there is a conclusion to your biography.

8. Choose a title for your biography.

9. Have an adult check it for you.

10. When you are happy with your work, copy your biography on good paper.

Writing: Descriptive Essay

When writing a descriptive essay, it is important that the descriptive essay:

- **has one clear dominant impression, whether written in poetry or in prose.** For example, In "My Country", by Dorathea McKellar, the words "flooding rains" gives us an impression of rain <u>falling hard</u>. The following description of Australia
  " I love a sunburnt country
          A land of sweeping plains,
          Of ragged mountain ranges"
  describes <u>a beautiful land of many contrasts</u> .

- **can be either objective or subjective.** For example, a description of a kangaroo is objective, giving a <u>clear, factual description</u>. It could be made subjective by adding the writer's feelings about kangaroos.

- **enable the reader to visualize what is being described.** To show rather than to tell.

- **appeal to as many senses as possible.** We have five senses, i.e. what is seen, smelt, heard, felt and tasted.

- **has details that should be carefully selected to support the dominant impression.** Details that do not do this may be left out.

- **uses precisely chosen vocabulary**, carefully chosen adjectives and adverbs, along with precise use of nouns and powerful verbs to help make the reader feel that they are experiencing what they are reading.

To write, follow the steps below:

1. **Choose your topic.** Pick something specific like an event, a person or an animal and strive to write something interesting, new or unusual about it/him/her.

2. **Have one clear dominant impression, whether written in poetry or in prose,** that you want to leave in the reader's mind. A description gives us an impression of rain <u>falling hard</u>. The description of Australia is of <u>a beautiful land of many contrasts</u> and the last description gives us the impression of <u>a large, powerful animal with big feet</u>.

3. **Jot down facts** you want to include.

4. Decide which of these you will use. **Number them and write the outline** in order. Remember, you only want one dominant impression.

5. **Make up sentences using your ideas**, following the numbering sequence you have already given your ideas. Write these down.

6. **Write a rough draft** on a spare sheet of paper. Check your spelling, capitalization, etc., working through the checklist for Writing. When you are happy with your draft, copy it onto good paper. Do not forget to give it a title.

7. **Check your work.** Make any corrections necessary. Be sure you have a beginning, a middle and an end. Check there are at least two sentences

8. **Check you have provided enough details and descriptions** to enable your reader to have a complete and vivid perspective.

9. **Delete any unnecessary details.**

10. **Correct punctuation and capital letters where appropriate.** Make sure you have not included abbreviations.

11. **Write a final draft.**

Writing: Dialogue

A dialogue is a conversation between two or more people, especially in a play or story.

For example: "Hello Jim. How are you?" asked Bill.
"Fine, thank you," said Jim. "What about you?"
"Can't complain," replied Bill.

When writing a dialogue, there are a few rules that need to be followed.

1. **Use quotation marks to show the words spoken by the character.**
   For example, "Good day, mate!."

2. **Every time the speaker changes you must start a new line.**
   For example,
   "I have lost my dog. Have you seen him? " Jane called across the street.
   "No. I'm sorry," Mary called back. "He didn't come this way and I have been weeding for an hour."

3. **Make sure the reader knows who is speaking.**

4. **Use correct punctuation, capitalization and spacing.**

5. **Only write dialogue that is useful in helping move your story along.**
   In a story, unlike a movie or play, the dialogue is not the only means of explaining what is happening.

6. **Use a variety of verbs, not just asked or said.**
   For example, replied, questioned.

7. **Vary the placement of the verbs identifying the speaker.**
   For example, John said, "Come and play with me, David."
   "Sorry John. Not today. Mum wants me to help her," replied David.

8. **Use narrative sentences to show the character's acts, thoughts and perceptions. Don't just show the reader what is being said.**
   For example, As Frank quietly closed the door behind him, he heard his mother calling, "Will someone please grab the washing off the line for me? It has started to rain."

9. **Your dialogue should sound like ordinary speech. Do not include expressions like "huh!" or swear words.**

10. **Don't try to provide too much information at once.**

Writing: Expository or Explanatory

Explanatory writing will generally contain an explanation of how something operates or why something is the way it is, e.g., how clouds are formed or why is critical thinking vital?

The first step is to decide what is your **topic**. This then forms your **title**.

Research

Before you start you will need to do some research on your topic.

Here are some points to help you:

- Make a note of the title, author, date printed, publisher and place of publication, as well as any pages you wish to quote from.
- Read the section you are interested in carefully before making notes.
- Unless quoting, when an acknowledgement needs to be made, do not write word for word. Write an outline containing the main points or ideas.
- Never keep notes on scraps of paper. It is best to have an exercise book you can use for this purpose.

Ordering your notes

Before you proceed further look through your notes and re-organise them into a logical sequence. You can do this on a sheet of paper and copy it into your notebook later.

Also include:

- any definitions you will need
- any key words
- (in your notebook) a bibliography
- any quotes you think are important

Introduction

Like any other essay an explanation begins with an introduction. The introduction contains a general statement that identifies what is being explained. It may include a definition or question.

- How are clouds formed? They are formed by microscopic drops of water or ice crystals settling on particles of dust. Each cubic metre of air will contain 100,000,000 droplets.

The Body

The body is made up of several paragraphs consisting of details, facts and examples.

For example, in the case of an explanatory essay that **describes** how something happens the following questions may be asked:

- what makes this happen?

- what is necessary for this to happen?
- how does everything work together?
- what is the result?

In the case of an explanatory essay that **asks why** something happens, the following questions may be asked:

- how and why does it start?
- what sequence does it follow and why? (This will probably be several paragraphs.)
- what results and why?

Further information on Explanatory Writing

- explain your important points in a logical order.
- use a new paragraph for every new point
- use the present tense
- write in an impersonal second or third person
- use technical vocabulary when necessary
- use vocabulary that shows cause and effect, e.g., because, therefore, as a result of, consequently
- pictures or diagrams to help illustrate your text (include in final copy)

Conclusion

The conclusion will summarise what has previously been said and state the result or consequence.

Edit

This is a very important step and should not be skipped through quickly.

As well as the checklist found in this book you should also check that:

- each paragraph focuses on one idea
- a topic sentence begins each new paragraph
- the entire essay has been written in the present
- the entire essay is in the second or third person
- the vocabulary is suitable for the topic—technical terms used when necessary

Hint: When you think your essay is completed, read it aloud, either to yourself or an audience. This makes it easier to identify mistakes.

Completing your Work

Write or type the final copy and add any pictures or diagrams.

Footnotes need to be used if you quote directly from a reference. It should include the name of the book, the author and the page number.

Your bibliography should appear as a separate page at the back of your work, It should include: name of the book, author, date, publisher and city published.

Writing: Invitation

Before you write an invitation you must ask yourself the following questions:

Who is being invited? A family or just a friend.

What? What are you inviting people to: a barbecue, a dinner, a party?

Where? Where is it being held?

When? When is it being held?

Why? What is the reason: a birthday, a get-together?

How? People want to know how to dress. If it is a barbecue, the dress will be casual but if it is a party the dress will be more formal.

Often at the bottom the letters **R.S.V.P.** will appear. This is French for reply if you please.

Below is a very simple invitation. Invitations are often sent on a card. Read the invitation carefully to see how the questions above have been included.

When you receive an invitation, it is very rude not to answer it even if you cannot attend. Parties need to be prepared and the host or hostess need to know exactly how many people are coming.

John Smith's 60th Birthday Party

To: The Jones Family | Who? |

Please come and help us celebrate the 60th Birthday of John Smith. | What? | | Why? |

Where: 56 Yandaloo Place, Smithton Vic 3757 | Where? |

When: 21st July 20014, 5pm - 11pm | When? |

A buffet meal will be provided. Please bring soft drinks. | How? |

R.S.V.P. by 30th June 20014 to Mary Smith, 40 Glenelg Crt, Westhampton, Vic 3756 or phone 57289656.

Writing: Invitation (Answering)

While many invitations, such as the ones on the previous page include a phone number, it is polite to send a written reply when you receive a written invitation.

Remember, every letter must have a heading, a date, a greeting, a body, a close and a signature.

The Heading
This contains your address as you are the person writing the letter.

52 Smith St,
Westhampton, Vic, 3757 | Date

20th June, 2014

| Greeting

Dear Mary,

Thank you for your kind invitation. Jane, Peter, John, Rosemary and I will be pleased to come and celebrate Uncle John's | Body | 60th birthday on 21st July with you.

If we can help in any way with the preparation and set up, please let us know.

Kind regards to all,

Veronica Jones. | Close

| Signature

There are some things that are important to remember when answering an invitation:

1. Reply to the name and address written beside the R.S.V.P.

2. Mention the date of the party.

3. Reply on behalf of the person or persons invited. In this case all of the Jones family were invited, so the reply must be on behalf of the whole family. Instead of "Jane, Peter, John, Rosemary and I" you could have written, "The Jones family."

4. A different close could be used, e.g., "Yours sincerely", "Your friend" or "With regards".

Writing: Letter (Business)

A business letter has a different format to a letter written to a friend. The letter is written more formally and a business letter includes both your address and the business you are writing to.

Read carefully through the letter below.

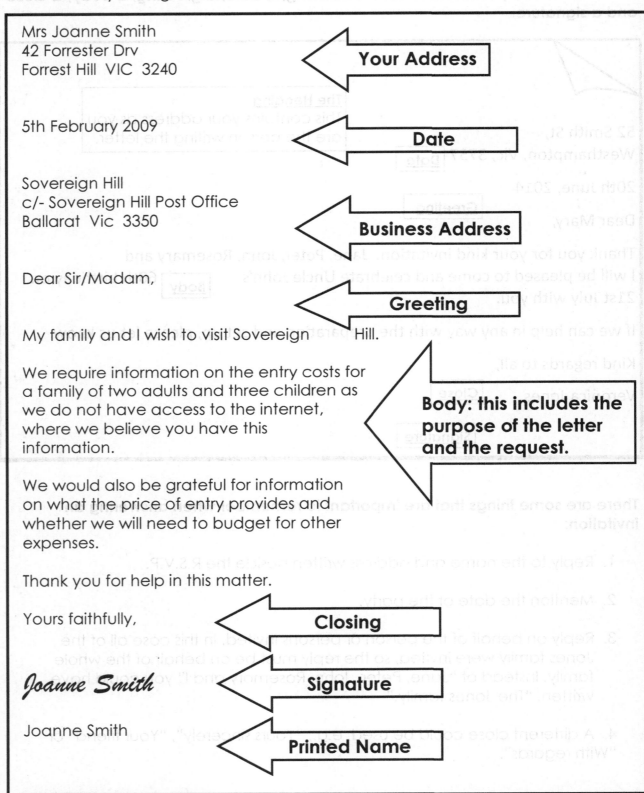

Mrs Joanne Smith
42 Forrester Drv
Forrest Hill VIC 3240

Your Address

5th February 2009

Date

Sovereign Hill
c/- Sovereign Hill Post Office
Ballarat Vic 3350

Business Address

Dear Sir/Madam,

Greeting

My family and I wish to visit Sovereign Hill.

We require information on the entry costs for a family of two adults and three children as we do not have access to the internet, where we believe you have this information.

Body: this includes the purpose of the letter and the request.

We would also be grateful for information on what the price of entry provides and whether we will need to budget for other expenses.

Thank you for help in this matter.

Yours faithfully,

Closing

Joanne Smith

Signature

Joanne Smith

Printed Name

© Valerie Marett and Carmel Musumeci
Coroneos Publications

Australian Homeschooling #567
English Handbook

Writing: Narrative

A narrative is a story told from a particular point of view, usually the author's, so there is the feeling of the author being involved in the story. A narrative contains a setting, character, plot, climax and ending. It is filled with <u>precise details</u> and uses <u>vivid verbs</u> to support it. It may use a dialogue.

A narrative contains:

Setting

Where and when does it take place? Ideas for setting the scene. Will the setting change later? Where to? How?

Characters: what characters are involved in the story?

Plot

Main events leading up to climax; climax possibly through complication or conflict; resolution; decreasing tension; closing.

General characteristic of a plot include:

    a. introduction—who? where? when?

    b. rising action—a dilemma or problem which disrupts the normal life or comfort of a character or characters and sets off a sequence of interesting events.

    c. climax

    d. slowing down of action

    e. conclusion or resolution

- conflict

- characterisation

- setting

- theme

- point of view

- sequence of events

Ideas can be expanded that you have written down into a rough draft under the following headings:

1. Introduction or Setting

The introduction introduces to you the character. This will be your first paragraph. The first sentence, sometimes called the "Topic Sentence," should capture the reader's attention.

2. Plot

—events that took place. The story should tell the main events leading to a climax. Include the problem or conflict.

3. Climax

The most important or exciting part of the story.

4. Conclusion or ending.

5. Re-read your draft copy.

Can you add more vivid verbs to increase the tension leading to the climax? Use the check list to correct your draft. When you are completely happy with your work, copy it into your workbook or write it on a separate sheet of paper and attach it.

Check the following

You need to review your narrative with the following points in mind. It may require redrafting your work several times. This does not matter. You may take several days to complete the work.

a. **characterisation**: do your people appear real?

- Have you included a description of their appearance? (Don't over do it. Make it brief.)
- Any idiosyncrasies?
- qualities: older, wiser, foolish
- Once you know your character, then you will know how they would act in a particular situation.

b. **setting**: this includes

- time
- location—where?
- circumstances: where they happen, e.g., I left the shopping centre
- when they happen: I left the shopping centre after collecting a parcel.
- It may even include a cultural background, e.g., visiting a relative overseas.

c. **The mood**—writers colour their writing with a certain mood or atmosphere which may change as events unfold. For example, the day may start well and then a catastrophe happens, e.g., the character falls off a bike. The mood will change to sad and scary depending on how hurt the character was.

It may also include:

- emotion: how people feel—happy, sad, etc.
- sight: what a thing looks like, what colour it is etc.
- sound: e.g., rustling, creaking, laughing
- touch: e.g., smooth pebbles, soft feel of a baby in your arms
- smell: acrid smell of smoke from the camp fire
- taste: sharp taste of a lemon drink on a dry throat

d. **theme:** the theme is the central idea of the story that is woven throughout and the character's actions, reactions and motivations all reflect this.

Go back and check your narrative and make sure that it is woven throughout.

e. **point of view:**
   - if written in the first person narrator, then the narrator is also the character and "I" will be used.
   - if written in the third person every character is referred to as "he", "she", "them", "we", "you".

f. **sequence of events:** the order of events helps you understand what you are reading, so it is important that it is logical.

Writing: Persuasive - An Advertisement

- An advertisement tells people what they need, want or would like to know.
- It will answer questions like who, what, why where, when and how.
- It will need to be interesting and draw the reader's eye and persuade them to read on.

You will need to:

- Make sure anyone reading your advertisement knows exactly what you are selling.

- Include an answer to questions like who, what, why, when, where or how?

- Add pictures to make the advertisement attractive.

Follow these steps:

1. Choose a topic.

2. Jot your ideas down.

3. Think of adjectives that might help get across your point, e.g., <u>largest toy</u> shop.

4. Decide on a heading.

5. Decide which ideas to include.

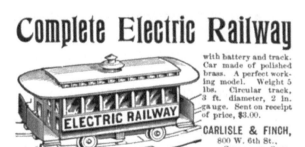

6. Try your ideas on a sheet of paper - keep your words to the smallest amount that will convey your message.

7. Have someone read your advertisement to make sure that they know what you are advertising.

8. When you are happy with your draft, copy it to a clean sheet of paper.

9. Add pictures.

10. Once you are sure you have finished, pin your advertisement up so others can see it or glue it into the back cover of your book.

Writing: Persuasive-Argumentative

There are many uses for persuasive writing. It can be used in a debate, and also in a newspaper. In a newspaper it is often referred to as a Commentary. The commentary usually appears on the same page as the Editorial, the comment by the Editor, or on the page before the Editorial.

The purpose of these commentaries is to present a compelling argument about a subject and convince the reader to agree with the writer's point of view. In a paper such as "The Australian" several commentaries may cover the same topic presenting several points of view. This allows the reader to form an opinion on important topics. These commentaries are generally about 1,000 words and the topic is presented in depth.

An argument has a set format, which is shown below:

- state the position
- argument 1
- argument 2
- argument 3 (further arguments can be included)
- conclusion—restate position

To present an argument:

- first research the facts.
- write an outline.
- expand the outline.
- make sure your argument is clear and precise.
- make only one argument per paragraph.
- write a draft copy.
- proof it and write the final copy.

Debate

A **debate** is a discussion where two teams of speakers put their views on a particular topic. The argument would be prepared in a similar manner but each person on the team would present only one argument. They would generally also try to rebuff the argument made by the other team.

Writing: Persuasive-Letter to the Editor

Newspapers contain letters written by the general public to the newspaper commenting on various issues which can vary widely. The most common topics include:

- supporting or opposing an editorial stance

- responding to another writer's letter to the editor

- commenting on current issues being debated by the Federal or State Parliaments

- remarking on a news story that appeared in a previous issue, either critically or positively

- correcting a perceived error or misrepresentation

Letters to the Editor are usually required to be <u>no more than 200 words</u>.

An effective persuasive letter will only result after consideration of the following points, although not all may apply in every situation:

- What is the idea, issue or change you are promoting?

- Who is the intended audience? What are the beliefs, problems and preferences of your audience?

- What possible objections may prevent your reader from responding favourably?

- What questions are likely to be asked about your proposed change or idea?

- What benefits can the reader gain from accepting your idea? How can you best demonstrate these benefits?

- What specific action do you want the reader to take and when do you want them to take it?

- How can you best attract and sustain your reader's attention?

- How can you convince your reader you are honest, logical and sincere?

Choose a topic and then draft your letter. In your first sentence you need to establish a bond with the reader, a central appeal which serves as a foundation on which to build your case. Look carefully at the example below.

Education

Education is a vital tool for equipping students for the workplace. A National Curriculum can deliver this, but it must be carefully planned and not rushed through.

Present your argument to convince your reader of what you are proposing.

The curriculum for each grade should be released a year at a time, ensuring that students have been taught the foundational material they need rather than dramatic changes being made to eleven grades at once. It is easy to write a curriculum that suggests that students should be able to identify, for example, phrases and clauses in year 8, but unless students have been taught how to identify the subject, predicate and object of a sentence in previous grades it will be impossible to accomplish.

Close by stating clearly the action you would like your readers to take.

I urge families concerned about the future education of their children to contact their local Members of Parliament and request that they take the necessary time to review the National Curriculum before implementing it.

Every letter to the editor must contain the following:

- full name and address
- a day time phone number for verification

Letters can usually be submitted:

- on-line
- by email
- by post
- by fax

When you send a letter to the editor you have agreed that the paper can edit your letter for legal reasons, lack of space or other reasons and may, after publication in the paper, republish it on the internet or media.

Proof read and correct your letter once again. Check it is not more than 200 words before sending a copy.

Writing: Poetry-Descriptive

Start by choosing a topic for your poem. Then complete the following:

1. Write down all the verbs you can think of that have to do with your topic,
   - Cats - purring, sleeping.

2. Write all the adjectives you can think of that have to do with your topic,
   - Cats - black, soft.

3. Look at the list of words you have written down. Think about how you can add another line that will rhyme with your first line. Two lines that rhyme together are called couplets. Write down your idea,

- I love my old black cat.
  You will often find him asleep on my mat.

4. Continue to write more lines that will follow on from your first ideas and will rhyme together. Use a piece of paper if needed.

5. Read through your lines of poetry. Change the order of the lines if you wish. Your poem may have two lines in each verse, four lines or however many you wish.

6. When you are happy with the results, write a good copy of your poem. You will find an extract from a descriptive poem below.

Great saffron sunset clouds, and larkspur mountains,
And fenceless miles of plain,
And hillsides gold-green in that unearthly
Clear shining after rain.
(extract from *Colour*, Dorothea McKellar)

Writing: Poetry- Limerick

A limerick is a funny poem of five lines that has both a rhythm and rhyme pattern.

Rhyme
The last word of the first, second and fifth lines rhyme with each other, e.g., in the limerick below:

One day I was wearing a sweater.
The weather was getting no better.
To say it quite plain,
It began to rain,
And I became wetter and wetter.

The words "sweater", "better" and "wetter" rhyme.

Rhythm
The first, second and fifth lines all have the same rhythm -
da Dum da da Dum da da Dum.

- one day I was wearing a sweater
  da Dum da da Dum da da Dum

The third and fourth line have a different rhythm -
da Dum da da Dum

- to say it quite plain

Ideas from limericks can be taken from anywhere. Follow some of the ideas below:

1. Choose a boy's or girl's name or a place.

   - There once was an old person of Fratton

2. Now make a list of words that rhyme with the last word,

   - hat on, pat on, sat on, mat on.

3. Write a second line using one of these words.

   - Who would go to church with his hat on.

4. Think of something interesting that might have happened to the person.

   - If I wake up, " he said, "With my hat on my head."

5. Choose another word that rhymes with the first line.

   - "I will know that it hasn't been sat on."

6. Write out the poem and check that the rhythm is correct by changing unstressed words to "da" and stressed words to "dum".

Writing: Poetry - Rhyming

Rhyming Poetry is a common form of poetry. It is pleasing to the ear and is often easier to remember. A repeating pattern also strengthens the form of the poem.

When the last word in a line of poetry rhymes with the last word in the next line the poem is said to be rhyming in couplets.

1. Write as many words that rhyme as you can think of,

   - ball, small, tall and fall.

2. Look at the words you have written. See if you can think of words that will turn these words into two lines of sentences.

3. Look at the lines of poetry that you have written. If any of them have a common idea, join them together to make four lines or think of other lines you can add.

   > I like to play with my new, red ball
   > Even though I'm very small.
   > Since I'm small I ride a tricycle

Writing: Nonsense Poems

Nonsense poems are just for fun. They do not have to make a great deal of sense. They aim to amuse the reader.

For example: **The Elephant**

> When people call this beast to mind,
> They marvel more and more
> At such a little tail behind,
> So large a trunk before
>
> *by Hilaire Belloc*

Follow these instructions carefully to write a nonsense poem. It does not matter if it is not very good. Just have fun doing it.

1. Think of what your poem will be about. If you can think of a story to tell in your nonsense poem it will make it better.

2. Write as many words as you can that rhyme with the words that you wish to use. Nonsense poems get their structure with rhyme.

   - blue, stew; day, way; walk, talk; fun, sun; look, took.

   Words that rhyme have the same ending sound.

   - hat and cat; plate and ate.

3. Then think of sentence that can use those words,

   - The dog turned all **blue**,
     When he ate the old **stew**.

     or
     While I played and had **fun**,
     The clouds came over the **sun**.

4. Re-read your story. Take out anything that is unnecessary or impedes the flow of the rhyme.

5. Here is an example of a nonsense poem with a story. It is called "How Doth the Little Crocodile" by Lewis Caroll.

   > How doth the little crocodile
   >   Improve his shining tail,
   > And pour the waters of the Nile
   >   On every golden scale!
   >
   > How cheerfully he seems to grin,
   >   How neatly spreads his claws,
   > And welcomes little fishes in,
   >   With gently smiling jaws.

Poetry: Understanding

Poets and their times

Poets reflect the events and ideas of their times through their poetry. An understanding of the time the poetry was written may lead to an understanding of the poet's ideas. Knowledge of the poet's background also gives us an insight.

1. Analysing Poetry

- Every poem will have a **theme** or main idea. It will convey the **message** or **intentions** of the poet.

- It may be a **narrative** which tells a story, or a **lyric** which describes the personal feelings of the poet.

2. Form

- A poem is written in a particular form. Poems are usually written in lines and these may be grouped in stanzas (verses), although this is not necessarily so. Free verse has no restrictions.

  Sentence structure may be altered slightly in poetry and there are **enjambment** or run-on lines. These occur at the end of a line where there is no punctuation. The sense continues into the next line and the poet's thoughts remain unbroken.

3. Diction or Word Choice

The poet's use of words creates the mood or atmosphere and sets the poem in its correct context, that is, its correct time and place.

- Word choice can influence the rhythm of the poem.

- In a rhyming poem, appropriate word choice is crucial.

- Jargon and slang may be used for effect.

- The use of repetition is also an effective device.

4. Tone

- The tone of the poem will reveal the poet's subjective views and attitudes.

- The tone helps to create the desired mood or atmosphere. This is achieved by word choice, rhythm and the sound of words.

- As in literature, the tone may be friendly, scary, angry etc.

5. Rhythm

Poetry often has a rhythm or flow and in this way is similar to music.

- the rhythm sets the pace of the poem and should match the meaning.

- a slow rhythm would enforce a sombre meaning and a quicker pace rhythm could reflect a happier mood.

- poetic sound devices influence the pace and pause of the rhythm.

6. Rhyme

Rhyme depends on the sound, not sight, and is frequently used by poets. Two consequently rhyming lines are called a **couplet**.

> "There was an old woman, as I've heard tell,
>   She went to market her eggs for to sell;"

A four lined poem is called a **quatrain**.

> Piping down the valley wild,
> Piping songs of pleasant glee,
> On a cloud I saw a child,
> And he laughing said to me,
> *"Happy Songs" by William Blake*

N.B. Lines 1 and 3 rhyme and lines 2 and 4.

7. Imagery

Imagery, often involving the senses, conjures up word pictures. It achieves this through a combination of literal and figurative language.

8. Metre

Metre is the number of stresses or beats in a line of poetry.

> He clasps/ the crag/ with crooked/hands:
> Close/to the sun/ in lonely/ lands,
> Ringed/ with the azure/ world,/ he stands.
> *"The Eagle" by Lord Tennyson*

Metre creates special effects to suit the mood of the poem. It can give a physical effect or create movement as in the last line of the poem above, "And/like a thunderbolt,/ he falls".

9. Poetry Terms

a. Personification: personification is a comparative figure of speech where inanimate (non-living) objects are given human qualities.

> The fire ran wild.

Fire can not run, it burns, but here it is given the human characteristic of running.

b. Symbolism: We constantly encounter symbolism in our daily lives. Perhaps the most commonly known symbols are the "$" sign that represents amounts of money and "M" for MacDonald's.

A symbol in poetry refers to the use of a specific, concrete item to stand for one or more concrete ideas. The grim reaper for example is used to portray death.

The following extract, on the next page, from a poem by William Blake contains symbolism.

A Poison Tree

> I was angry with my friend:
> I told my wrath, my wrath did end.
> I was angry with my foe:
> I told it not, my wrath did grow.

A tree is a symbol of growth and development. Poison is the symbol of death and destruction. By placing the two words together William Blake shows how the growth of suppressed anger in a relationship grew like a tree.

Below are some further examples of symbolism.

- black is used to represent death or evil.
- white stands for life and purity.
- red can symbolise blood, passion, danger or an immoral character.
- purple represents royalty.
- yellow often stands for violence and decay.
- blue represents peacefulness and calm.
- a chain can symbolise the coming together of two things.
- a ladder may represent the relationship between heaven and earth.
- roses stand for romance.
- violets represent shyness.
- lilies represent beauty and temptation.
- chrysanthemums represent perfection.

c. **Onomatopoeia**: this is a figure of speech used to describe a word that imitates or suggests the source of the sound it describes, e.g., tick tock.

Onomatopoeia is frequently used in nursery rhymes, e.g., Twinkle, Twinkle, Little Star; Baa, Baa, Black Sheep.

Onomatopoeia is shown in this example from "The Rime of the Ancient Mariner" by S.T. Colderifge

> The ice was here, the ice was there,
> The ice was all around:
> It cracked and growled and roared and howled
> Like noises in a swound!

The words cracked, growled, roared and howled are all examples of onomatopoeia.

d. **Alliteration**: the repetition of consonants, especially at the beginning of words is called alliteration. Some poets use it to create rhythmic or musical effects; other poets use it to focus the reader's attention on certain qualities or attributes.

An example of alliteration is shown in the familiar tongue twister: Peter Piper picked a peck of pickled peppers.

Writing: Procedures

The purpose of this genre is to show how something might be accomplished. People need to have a system or sequence to follow when they are learning to **make** or to **do** something, e.g., cook a cake, play a board game, take a telephone message or even in response to a query, direct someone to a place.

When using this genre, always choose a topic you know something about or research a subject which interests you.

Start with a rough copy. Only write a good copy when you have insured your instructions work.

1. List the items you will need, e.g., ingredients in a cake or the equipment included, e.g., a board game might include board, counters, cards or dice.

2, Note any previous knowledge that will be needed before starting, e.g., before sewing a garment the reader should have knowledge of how to use a sewing machine.

3. Number steps in the order they must be carried out. Do not include more than one activity in each step.

4. Leave a space between each step.

5. Illustrations may help the reader understand better. For example: paste the ends of two strips of paper together to form a right angle or square corner.

6. Use vocabulary suitable to the subject matter and the intended audience. If necessary define the terms used.

5. Reread the instructions you have written carefully. Make any alterations necessary.

6. Have someone with no knowledge of what you are trying to teach follow the instructions, e.g., a younger child. Make any corrections necessary.

Making a Cup of Coffee

You will need:
kettle, water, cup, teaspoon, coffee, milk and sugar.

Method:
a. Make sure there is at least 1 cup of water in the kettle.
b. Boil the water.
c. While the water is boiling, place 1 teaspoonful of coffee in a cup.
d. Fill the coffee cup 3/4 full of boiling water.
e. Add milk and sugar to suit personal taste.

Writing: Recount

a. Ask yourself before writing:
   ⇒ What happened?
   ⇒ Who was present?
   ⇒ When did it happen?
   ⇒ What caused it?

b. List any ideas you have that are about the topic. They do not need to be in sentences.

c. Organize your ideas from A and B into order and jot them down on a piece of paper.

d. Make up sentences using your ideas and write them on scrap paper.

e. Edit your story then have an adult check it for you.

f. When you are happy with the results, write your story out neatly and illustrate it if there is room for a picture in your book.

Writing: Science Experiment

Scientists write up each experiment they undertake. It enables them to see what progress they have made and also prove any results to the scientific community.

Experiments should always be written up showing:

Aim: the purpose of the experiment.

Equipment: what equipment you need to undertake the experiment, e.g., flask, water etc.

Method: each step taken to conduct the experiment.

Result: there may be one result or, for example, in a biological experiment, it may require days or weeks of written results.

Conclusion: has your experiment enabled you to come to a conclusion? In some cases it may take many experiments to reach a conclusion.

This experiment provides an example:

The **aim** of the experiment is to see:
   a. which appears first, the roots or the leaves.
   b. how long it takes for leaves to develop other than the cotyledon s) contained within the seed.

You will need:
container, sponge to fit inside of dish, water, corn and pea seeds.

Method:

    a. Place the sponge in the dish

    b. Add water until the sponge is rising above the water level.

    c. Place corn seeds on one end of the sponge and pea seeds on the other.

    d. Place the container in a sunny location.

    e. Ensure water level is topped up from time to time.

Results
Use a chart similar to the following:

	Corn	Peas
Day 1	_____	_____
Day 2	_____	_____

Conclusion:
Analyse your results and write your conclusion.

Writing: Scientific or Technical Report

A scientific or technical report is far more than a few pages written on a topic. It is a detailed report of sometimes hundreds of pages and takes time to complete.

What is contained in a technical report?

- a title page
- numbered pages (all of them)
- a table of contents
- a summary
- it is written on one side of the page only
- it is divided into sections and sub-sections and arranged logically under appropriate headings
- a logical numbering system for the headings, sub-headings etc.
- each main heading must start on a new page
- introduction
- conclusion and/or recommendations
- appropriate numbering and labelling system for diagrammes used
- footnotes where applicable
- appendices where applicable
- a bibliography or list of references
- presented in a folder which will also display a title—the presentation and summary define the difference between professional and amateur reports

There are two main parts to writing a technical report. These are:

- collecting and arranging information

- presenting information as a report

1. Outline the Topic:

Two examples are given below: N.B. This type of report will take many weeks to complete. It may be used in Universitys or TAFE's when presenting a thesis, or in business, when presenting a proposal. Examples of the two types and what might be included in the research are shown below.

Technical Report
Purpose: The feasibility of an ornamental pool in a back yard.
- a. legal requirements
- b. size of the pond
- c. location of pond
- d. design and layout of the pond
- e. cost of pond
- f. types of plants and fish to be used in the pond
- g. safety considerations, e.g., noxious plants, protection of fish from predators, protection for children to avoid drowning.

Scientific Report
Purpose
To identify the best method of keeping chickens (in a backyard) and whether it is feasible.
- a. legal requirements, e.g., council or borough regulations
- b. economics of buying eggs against keeping chickens
- c. free range or restricted movement—in fenced run
- d. best type of chickens to keep
- e. home for the chickens. (Most chickens are locked up at night to protect them. They also have a nesting box making egg collection easier.)
- f. safety requirements: protection from predators, provision to stop birds escaping
- g. health requirements: cleanliness of the area they live in, removal of droppings, reduction of odour
- h. reduction of vermin

2. Researching These Types of Reports
- a. **Sources of Information:** these include local government bodies, books, magazines and newspapers, internet, lectures, films, T.V. and radio programmes, experiments, surveys, interviews, investigations,

- b. **Laboratory and Field Work:** this may be original work and development, experiments, tests or research into new methods and apparatus. The most significant results should be selected for inclusion. This work may sometimes be performed by the writer of the report and at other times be observed by the writer depending on the nature of the result.

3. Recording Information

Eventually the information must be written down. Always record where the information came from. One way to do this is to keep all notes obtained from one reference together in a folder with clear indication of details of the reference, e.g., to identify the best method of keeping chickens. **If you store any work at all on a computer always back it up on an alternate source. Always keep hard copies of any notes you make.**

At the top of each set of notes write in full details of the resource that is being used, i.e., in the case of a **book**— the **author, title, publishing date, publisher** and **where published**. If you are using the **internet** keep a note of the **website, title** and **author**.

As you write the notes keep a note of the **number of the page** from which each item is obtained. Use abbreviation wherever possible as long as you can understand them later on.

If you are copying from a book or article word for word indicate with inverted commas. If you wish to leave out a section of the quote show this by the use of dots .... If you wish to insert words not included, place them in brackets.

Try to include material that is relevant only to your purpose. If you are not sure write it down. It will be easier to leave out later than go back to the text and try to find it again.

4. Select Relevant Material

a. Start with the most important point in your research. In the case of the topic given for both the science and technical report, the most important question is the legality of the project. In the case of the technical report there is likely to be a limit on the size of the ornamental pond and as there are water safety issues that must be considered. In the case of the science report the main legal issue is likely to be the number of chickens and how they must be kept. You must therefore start by researching these issues with your local council or borough. If there is relevant legislation this needs to be attached in the appendage.

b. Use selective reading. Skim through material to locate a particular detail or reference and then read the material carefully.

c. Take notes:
    i.   read the passage to obtain a general impression.
    ii. check the meaning of unknown or difficult words.
    iii. re-read carefully making a mental note.
    iv. make a note of the parts that seem important and relevant. Copy any comments you may wish to quote. Note the name of the book, author and page reference.
    v.   re-read the reference material to make sure it has been understood and notes are accurate.

d. Take notes:
   i. read the passage to obtain a general impression.
   ii. check the meaning of unknown or difficult words.
   iii. re-read carefully making a mental note.
   iv. make a note of the parts that seem important and relevant. Copy any comments you may wish to quote. Note the name of the book, author and page reference.
   v. re-read the reference material to make sure it has been understood and notes are accurate.

A number of readers may look at a report. Some may want only the conclusions; others may read the summary, which has the gist of the report; and yet others may want to read the report in full. It is important you cater for these various needs.

The Elements of the Report

While we are dealing individually with various parts of the report, each section must hang together, complementing and reinforcing each other.

1. The Title Page

This is the first contact the reader will have with the report. It should contain:

- the title of the report
- the author's name
- the name of the person authorising the report
- the date
- the names of the people to whom the report is to be circulated (if necessary)

The title should be brief, but descriptive and should give the reader a clear indication of the subject.

2. Summary

This provides a brief run-down of the main points of the report section by section. It will deal only with points made in the report. From the summary the reader should be able to grasp what the report is about and to gain the most essential information.

3. Table of Content

This is the key to the report as it will enable the reader to find his way around the report with the least possible effort. A glance should enable him to find the whereabouts of any specific piece of information he requires.

The paragraph/section number should be clear and so should include the subject heading.

Section Number	Subject	Page
1.0	Introduction	1
1.1	Aims	2
1.2	Scope	2

Introduction

The introduction should supply the reader with any necessary background, state the aim or purpose of the report and outline the scope of the report that is, give a clear idea of the points to be dealt with in the report.

Background

This will give the reader a brief indication of the history, e.g., why you decided to build a pond and a brief history of its uses in gardens.

Aim

The reason you are writing the report. What is the aim? Is it to describe something, tell the reader how to make something, to compare one method against another?

Scope

This should be an outline of your approach; the points you are going to deal with. In other words it should supply the reader with a map of where you will be taking him.

5. The Body of the Report

All the points referred to in the introduction will be taken up and discussed in full. The heading will not be "Body. " It might be for example:

1.0 Council Regulations

2.0 Breeds and Numbers of Chickens

3.0 Housing

Clear headings are essential. Use major headings and sub-headings.

The subject of the report should be dealt with in logical order and it should be easy for the reader to follow your argument or description step by step.

Deal with only one thing at a time. It is always best to give the reader a general picture first, then move on to particulars. For example, if you are building something, start off with the complete aspect first and if possible draw a diagram: then use sub-headings to deal with particular aspects.

6. Conclusion

In the conclusion the report is wound up. Main points or arguments can be repeated and conclusions or recommendations reiterated. This will reinforce the reader's understanding of the report. It is important to hammer home the essential findings of the report so that the reader remembers what you have actually recommended.

© Valerie Marett and Carmel Musumeci
Coroneos Publications

Australian Homeschooling #567
English Handbook

7. Presentation

Careful attention needs to be paid to the arrangement and presentation of the final report. (We will deal more with this later.) No matter how important the content of a report is, a report that is badly presented will fail in its purpose.

Generally, people who will read your reports when you are working or lecturers in further education have a lot of material they need to review. They expect that anyone who wishes to get their attention with written material will make their material attractive and as easy to read as possible. This will enable the reader to get the information they need as easily and as quickly as possible.

Making An Outline

Sort the material you have collected and then select what you want to include. Organise it into a logical sequence. This outline then acts as a map that will help you achieve unity and coherence. It is a skeleton that shows the relationship between the various topics or aspects discussed in the report and their relationship to the broad, overall subject. Furthermore, the headings of the outline automatically furnish the numbers or letters, in proper sequence, for the table of contents. The mechanical structure of the outline shows which aspects are more important (headings) and which are less important (sub-headings).

Forming an Outline

There is a set format that needs to be followed. You may use letter-number or the decimal form.

Letter—Number

First Order or Principal items are labelled with capital Roman numerals, e.g., I, II, III, IV, V.

- Second Order use capital letters, e.g., A, B, C.
- Third Order use the Arabic numerals, e.g., 1, 2, 3, 4.
- Fourth order use lower case letters, e.g., a, b, c, d.
- Fifth order use lower case Roman numerals, e.g., i, ii, iii, iv.
- Sixth order use lower case letters in brackets e.g., (a), (b), (c).

Decimal Forms

- First order items are labelled with whole numbers, e.g., 1.0; 2.0; 3.0;
- Second order use a number one decimal place e.g., 1.1; 2.1.
- Third order use a number plus two decimal places, e.g., 1.1.1; 2.4.1.

Below is a short example:

1. **Introduction**
   1.1 Aim: to investigate the best pet and the conditions necessary to keep them
   1.2 Scope:
   1.2.1 pets suitable for size of garden
   1.2.2 number of pets

Australian Homeschooling #567
English Handbook

2. **Council Regulations:**..

3. **Details of housing etc needed for pets**
    1.1   run for cats
    1.2   kennel for dog

4. **Conclusions**...

Writing A Rough Draft

A rough draft will produce the first version of the report. It is derived from the notes and data collected earlier. It may be considered a "fleshing out" of your outline and will be polished later.

Hints

- begin immediately.

- write rapidly. Delays result in omissions of material and loss of continuity.

- check any points that are unclear.

- follow the outline from beginning to end unless you have a reason for preparing a sequence or section out of order, e.g., an appendix or biography.

- be sure to transcribe your first draft from notes where possible.

- double space sentences to allow corrections and additions to be written between the lines.

- **back up your material and print a hard copy if you need to stop.**

- write any corrections, insertions, erasures etc. on your printed page to suit yourself but make sure you can read the draft. You can make changes on the computer later.

- if someone else is going to read your rough draft, print out a fresh copy for them. Never ask someone to read a draft on the computer.

- refer freely to illustrations and supplementary material. You should already have selected appropriate illustrations and planned others during the preliminary stage. You should have also planned and produced any charts and tables necessary. Assign numbers, even if temporarily, e.g., Fig. 1; Chart A; Table 5 etc. Refer to these numbers as you write the rough draft, e.g., list of pets and numbers that may be kept in the suburbs are given in Table B.

- keep your list of references nearby so that you can refer to the entries as you write your rough draft.

- number the pages of the draft consecutively.

- check the completed draft against your outline and notes to make sure there have been no omissions and that all points have been adequately discussed.

- leave for a day and then check again.

Footnotes

Footnotes appear in a separate section at the bottom of the page. They are written in different print, usually italics, and give additional information regarding some part of the work appearing on the page.

A recognisable mark, usually a small number or an asterisk, is placed immediately following that part of the work. The same mark is placed in the footnote section of the page and is followed by the footnote, e.g., poodles[2]
For example: [2] *Smith, John: Breeds of Dogs, Hamlyn, 2008 p. 35*

If numbers are used to identify the footnote they start from 1 on each new page.

There are two types of footnotes:

- this type gives the source of the information regarding some part of the main work.
- the second type gives the source of a quotation, fact or opinion. **All** quotation marks must acknowledge the origin. It is a matter of judgement to decide which facts and/or opinions should be supported by reference to their origin. Fairly obvious ones like World War I started in 1914 do not require it. Ones that might be disputed like William the Conqueror slipped on the stones when he landed at Hastings in 1066, should be supported.

Points to Remember

- Footnotes should give full details, i.e., author, title, publisher, date of publication, page number in that order.
- "Ibid" is an abbreviation of "ibidem" meaning from the same book/chapter, passage as directly above. This saves writing out the name, author etc. again.
- It is not possible to use ibid where there is a footnote referring to another reference between the two quotes. Instead you must use "op. cit." which is an abbreviation of "opere citato" meaning in the work already quoted. The author's name is included to avoid any other previously mentioned references, e.g., John Smith, op. cit., p. 35.

Completing the Technical or Scientific Report

Revising and Rewriting
This should be completed slowly.

Check the following:

- are there any technical inaccuracies?
- are all statements you have made true?
- is the content clearly presented or is it puzzling?
- logic: is the sequence meaningful?
- are statements and claims adequately supported?
- are the conclusions valid?
- do the recommendations make sense?
- are the conclusions valid?
- can you find any fault in the outline?
- grammar, spelling, sentence structure, sentence variety, style, etc.

Repeat the process of refinement. Ask a friend to read and check it.

Preparing the Final Draft

All material will have been revised several times at this stage, although further modifications are likely.

Assemble all material. Organise it according to the following format:
- Summary
- Table of Contents
- Introduction
- Background
- Aim
- Scope
- The Main Body of the Report
- Conclusion
- Appendix
- Bibliography

Remember your report is to be single sided.

To be able to write the table of contents you will need to assemble your report and then make sure that every page is numbered, and although the numbers need not appear on the pages containing the summary and table of content, they will still need to be given a number, e.g., Table of Contents is page 2 so Introduction will be page 3, etc.

Make sure your report contains a cover and is presented beautifully. Presentation is extremely important and can make the difference between your report being read or ignored.

Writing a Story

Most stories have a beginning, a middle and an end.
- The beginning tells who the main people are and where the story takes place.
- The middle tells the main part of the story.
- The end rounds off the story.
- Stories are written in paragraphs. Each paragraph must have one main idea and be at least three sentences long.

Remember: A paragraph contains one main idea.

Before we write a story, we must ask some questions:
- Who? (the character): this may be a person, animal or thing, for example, a teddy bear.
- What? (the plot): the main event that happens in the story.
- Where? (the setting): the place and time where the story occurs.

- when? (the period): the time when it was written, e.g., today or fifty years ago.

Remember: follow the steps outlined.

1. Write your ideas about your story on a rough sheet of paper.

2. Organise your thoughts into order.

3. Expand your thoughts to form paragraphs. Do not forget you need a beginning, middle and end. The middle may be more than one paragraph. (look at How to Write a Paragraph and follow the instructions.)

4. Edit your work. Rewrite it neatly in an exercise book. Keep this book to store your completed stories and other written work.

5. You may illustrate your work if you wish and **add a title**.

Writing: Story - Beginning

The beginning is very important. This is the start of your story and it needs to catch your reader's attention, so they will want to go on reading.

- Think carefully about your topic.
- Make sure it tells who the main people are and where the story takes place.

Writing: Story - Ending

- The ending of a story is important.
- It should bring the story to a natural conclusion, which leaves the reader feeling the story is finished and complete.
- It should draw the story together and complete the telling of the events.

Story Writing - An Adventure Story

The object of a story is to provide entertainment for the reader. Stories can be based on truth or be totally fiction. The characters in an adventure story are more realistic, unlike the "Tall Story" where they are greatly exaggerated. Blinky Bill is an example of an animal adventure story.

The process for writing a story or a tall story is similar. Refer back to the topic of Writing a Tall Story if you need to.

A. Choose a topic.

B. Summarise or outline your story.

C. Setting:

1. List possible settings for your story:

2. When does this story take place?

3. List other characters that are important to the story.

4. List any details to the setting that will be important as the story progresses. Do you move from a city to a mountain, for example?

D. Character(s):

1. Appearance
—what does your character look like? List adjectives that might be useful.

2. Action
—the actions of the character will show what type of a person he/she is. List the characteristics you want him/her to portray and then think how you will weave this into your story.

3. Speech
—your character's speech will reflect both his character and background.

4. Thoughts
—include some of your character's fears, hopes and memories.

E. Plot
The plot details the main events that happen in a story. Jot down ideas about some of events that will occur in your story.

F. Expand
Expand some of the ideas you have already written down under the following heading:

1. Introduction
The introduction introduces to you the character. This will be your first paragraph. The first sentence, sometimes called the "Topic Sentence" should capture your reader's attention. For example, Friday was the most exciting day of my life, yet it started like any other day.

2. **Middle or the Story**
   Events that took place.

3. **Climax**
   The most important or exciting part of the story.

4. **Conclusion or Ending.**

Look back over points 1—4. When you write use them as your guide, they will become your rough draft.

Check your rough draft for the following:

a. Is the main character clearly written? -appearance, feeling etc.

b. Does the story have a <u>beginning</u>, a <u>middle</u> and an <u>end</u>?

c. Does it have a dramatic climax?

d. Are you happy with your rough draft?

e. Also check your work for these:
   - Have you written about the topic?
   - Can adjectives or adverbs be added to make the story better?
   - Can you change the vocabulary to make it more vivid? (Use a thesaurus.)
   - Have some words been used too often?
   - Have words appropriate to the topic been used?
   - Have you used correct punctuation?
   - Are there capital letters at the beginning of each sentence?
   - Are there at least two sentences in each paragraph?
   - Is there a new paragraph for every new idea?
   - Is the spelling correct?
   - Does the story have a title?
   - Refer back to the checklist for further suggestions.

Do not try to rush through writing your story. Take your time. When you are happy with it, read it aloud to someone before writing the final copy. Correct any mistakes and then rewrite it neatly.

A Plot Chart (shown below) may help you map out your story more easily.

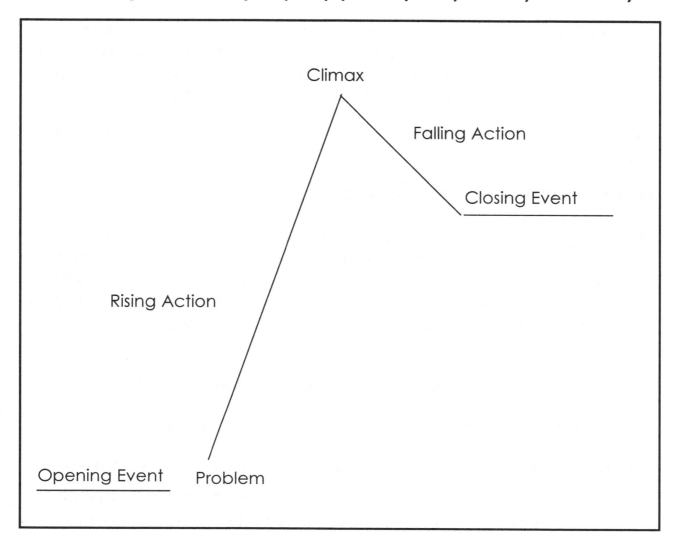

Opening Event
Setting, time and place of story, introduction of main character or characters.

Rising Action
The events and conflicts that happen before the climax of the story. This will include the problems that occur, disagreements or fights.

Climax
The highest point

Falling Action
Events that happen after the climax, bringing the reader to the close of the story.

Closing Event
Point at which all the loose ends of the story are tied together.

Writing a Tall Story

Every culture in the world has tall stories. Story telling was a means of entertainment before radio and television. People sat around campfires and told stories. In Australia, bushman vied with each other to tell stories and each time they repeated them, they embellished the story.

Think of the story you would like to tell. Discuss this with an adult so it is clear in your mind.

Write a few ideas, in sentences, concerning your story.

My example: Trevor the lion looks majestic. He has a timid roar that sounds more like a kitten than a lion. He often ran away when other animals appeared. One day hunters arrived and start capturing the animals. Trevor was frightened but he knew that he was the only one who could save them. He roared into a cave, which amplified his voice.

Stories are made up of **settings**, **characters** and **plots**. Below the explanations of these words are questions. These questions will help you to write your story, so jot down your ideas after each question.

A. **Setting** : the setting is the place and time where the story happens.

1. List possible settings for your story: (My example: the jungle)
2. When does this story take place? (My example: long, long ago)
3. List other animals or people that are important.
4. List any details that will be important as the story progresses. Does the time of day change, for example?

B. **Character** :the character in a story is the main person or thing. When we speak of the character we mean not only what he looks like, but how he thinks and what his behaviour is like.

1. What does your character look like? (My example: large, tawny lion, strong, powerful.)
2. How does he think or feel about himself and others? (My example: cowardly lion, afraid of other animals, lonely.)
3. How does he behave? (My example: lurks in the shadows, hides behind trees. At end of story—powerful, proud, well liked.)

C. **Plot**: the plot details the main events that happen in a story.

1. **How will the character react in different situations?**

My example: Hid behind trees when someone came. When hunters arrived, panicked and ran in circles. Had a bright idea—roared into cave.)

2. **Exaggeration and Improbability: in a Tall Story the events are greatly exaggerated and the unexpected happens.**

My example: in my story the lion became angry and roared into the entrance of a cave. The mountain and ground shook, the roar echoed louder and louder, picking up sound as it swept through the jungle. The lion's shadow was cast, making him look as large as a mountain.)

Write notes on some of the ways you can exaggerate your plot and characters.

Expand some of the ideas you have already written down. Make sure you have the following:

A. Introduction
The introduction introduces to you to the character. This will be your first paragraph. Remember, this is a Tall Story so the character will be exaggerated and larger than life.

B. Middle or Events that took place.

C. Climax
The most important or exciting part of the story.

D. Conclusion or Ending.

Look back over A-D. This is your rough draft. Check it through for grammar and punctuation. Can you add adjectives and verbs to make it more exciting? Can you change the vocabulary to make it more vivid? (Use your thesaurus.)

Work through the Writing Checklist. When you are happy with the result write a good copy.

© Valerie Marett and Carmel Musumeci
Coroneos Publications

Australian Homeschooling #567
English Handbook